DAY BY DAY WITH

J. B. PHILLIPS

DAY BY DAY WITH

J. B. PHILLIPS

*Selected Readings for
Daily Reflection*

Edited by
DENIS DUNCAN

HENDRICKSON
PUBLISHERS

Hendrickson Publishers, Inc.
P. O. Box 3473
Peabody, Massachusetts 01961-3473
ISBN 1-56563-726-7

The authors assert the moral right to be identified as the authors
of this work

Published by
The Bible Reading Fellowship
First Floor, Elsfield Hall
15-17 Elsfield Way, Oxford OX28FG
ISBN 1-84101-035-9

First published in Great Britain by Hodder and Stoughton
1983 edition published by Arthur James Ltd.

Acknowledgments
Extracts from the Authorized Version of the Bible (The King James Bible),
the rights in which are vested in the Crown, are reproduced by
permission of the crown's Patentee, Cambridge University Press.

Scripture quotations from the Jerusalem Bible, copyright © 1966 by
Darton, Longman & Todd Ltd and Doubleday & Company, Inc.

Printed and bound in Great Britain by Biddles Ltd,
Guildford and Kings Lynn
Hendrickson Publishers' edition reprinted by arrangement with
The Bible Reading Fellowship.
Hendrickson Edition First Printing — 2003

INTRODUCTION

In his autobiography, *The Price of Success*, J.B. Phillips writes, 'I think I must have been born a believer', but hastily adds, 'This does not mean that I was born a Christian.' He says that he was no more than three-and-a-half when he began to feel the vastness of the creation and hence of the Creator, and he remembers reflecting, 'If he stops thinking about me, I shall not exist at all.'

His childhood was a troubled one and for the last twenty years of his life he was in deep depression—emerging only occasionally to take up his pen in some Christian cause. Yet, all his life, in resounding success and in times of disappointment and failure, he held on to his faith in God. He would say, 'I know God may hurt me, but he will not harm me.' This strong faith in God was coupled with a longing to communicate it to others. In those twenty years of depression, he never failed to respond to a cry for help. His correspondence was immense and there are many who thanked God for the comfort he had given them. It was this compulsion to communicate even in the midst of his own misery that led his widow and me to call a collection of these letters, to be published as a book, *The Wounded Healer*.

TRANSLATING THE BIBLE INTO MODERN ENGLISH

J.B. Phillips will be remembered as the post-war pioneer of biblical translation into modern English. His first and most memorable success was *Letters to Young Churches*—a translation with introductions to all the epistles in the New Testament. The origin of that was in the youth club of his much-bombed church in London, in 1941. He argued that, as much of the New Testament was written to Christians in danger, it should be relevant to those young people 'who for many months lived in a different but no less real danger'. He could assume that they had some acquaintance with the Gospels, so he read from the epistles—Colossians at first—and it left them cold. They just did not understand the splendid language of the Authorized Version. The epistle meant much to him when he read it in Greek. So he attempted the task of translating it into language they could understand. And they did.

When he sent a copy of this translation of Colossians to the famous Christian writer, C.S. Lewis, he received an enthusiastic reply. 'Do the lot!' said C.S. Lewis, and he did. C.S. Lewis' reply on reading the first translation is worth quoting: 'I thought I knew Colossians pretty well but your paraphrase made it far more significant—it was like seeing a familiar picture after it's been cleaned.'

THE SWEETS OF SUCCESS

The success of *Letters to Young Churches* was phenomenal. After a slow start—1300 sold in the first nine months—it gradually picked up, until, in 1948, reviews in Britain, and even more so in America, boosted the sales to as many each week. This paraphrase had found its moment. The epistles, which had seemed obscure to many, now became clear and vibrant. J.B. Phillips had set himself three clear goals: write something that can be understood as 'English', not a translation from a foreign tongue; let it have its own style and, as a translator, avoid pressing your own personal style upon it; let it produce in the hearts and minds of its readers an effect equivalent to that produced by the author upon his original readers.

Faithful to the original text, but in the language of the day, it resounded through the English-speaking world. Later, Phillips went on to translate the rest of the New Testament—*The Young Church in Action* (The Acts of the Apostles), *The Gospels*, and *The Book of Revelation*. NTIME (*The New Testament in Modern English*) spread throughout the English-speaking world. The New Testament was now being read, not just bought. J.B. Phillips could communicate. The BBC recognized this and were soon asking him to broadcast; he was greatly in demand as a speaker throughout Britain and America. Soon he found that he could write books about the Christian life in a language that readers found free of religious jargon, and not confined in a religious worldview. The books were good reading and persuasive evangelism. They dealt with real problems that people wanted help with. The titles themselves tell us a great deal about his skills of communication: *Your God is Too Small*, *Is God at Home?*, *When God was Man*, *Appointment with God*, and many other titles. His broadcast talks on one occasion were published under the title *Plain Christianity*. They sold and were read. A vast correspondence ensued which went on well into his period of depression. Looking back, he described this period of success—and its price—in moving terms.

'I was in a state of some excitement throughout the whole of 1955. My work hardly seemed arduous for it was intrinsically exciting. I was tasting the sweets of success to an almost unimaginable degree, my health was excellent, my future prospects were rosier than my wildest dreams could ever suggest, applause, honour, appreciation met me wherever I went...'

THE DARK YEARS AND THEIR LESSONS

J.B. Phillips was still doing a fair measure of speaking in schools and churches until the late summer of 1961 and then, quite suddenly, his speaking, writing, and communicating powers stopped. He made two types of comment on that sudden collapse, which reveal as clearly as anything the ability of this man to write English that left no doubts about its meaning. First a description of the event: 'Without any particular warning the springs of creativity were suddenly dried up: the ability to communicate disappeared overnight and it looked as if my career as a writer and translator was over.' And then the explanation: 'I was not aware of the dangers of success. The subtle corrosion of character, the unconscious changing of values and the monstrous growth of a vastly inflated idea of myself seeped slowly into me. Vaguely I was aware of this.'

He struggled with one piece of translation work. Many had urged him to do the Old Testament and thus complete the Bible. He hesitated, partly because while he was much at home with Greek, he felt uncertain of his hold on Hebrew, a language he disliked! But urged and assisted, he produced *Four Prophets*, a translation of Amos,

Hosea, Micah and Isaiah 1—39. Although it does not have the high quality of the New Testament work, he did produce the finest translation of Micah I have ever read. A few years later, he was disturbed by the growing tendency in radio and, more especially, TV to call in question the basic teaching of the Church. The swinging '60s troubled him. One evening, watching a religious broadcast more or less dismissing the resurrection, he broke his silence on the question of the truth of the Bible. All his powers returned as he defended the Bible, not as a fundamentalist but as a translator who had spent years with the text of the New Testament and finding himself convinced of its truth. It had the ring of truth about it—and that was the title of a book that went into many editions: *The Ring of Truth*. It was first published in 1967—Phillips' last book, although he revised his translations during these dark years.

THE CORRESPONDENCE

Although he was not publishing, or accepting any public engagements, Phillips was conducting a pastoral work of immense proportions. All unaware of his desperate situation, readers of his books began to turn to him for pastoral help. Letters came from all over the world and he answered them all. Today they are in fifteen box files deposited in Dr Williams' Library, a theological library in central London with church archives, available for students for research and book borrowing. Some readers wrote about the way he had translated the New Testament and a correspondence ensued which threw much light on the text. Others were beginning to recover their faith after reading one of his books. Some of his responses were theological, others very personal. Almost always he was patient, explaining why he agreed or did not agree, carefully guiding the writer to a sane and stable view. He was a little impatient with some fundamentalists who had written to pin him down dogmatically. He could be angry with those who attempted to undermine others' faith. The correspondence is a mine of the troubles that beset the faithful in those disturbing times in the 1960s and '70s. Many wrote about dealing with their depression, unaware of what he was suffering. He also wrote himself to many outstanding Christian people about his depression, only to discover that some of them were in depression themselves or on the brink of it. Immediately, his pastoral concern returned and he began to help those to whom he had turned for help. Although some of these letters were included in *The Wounded Healer*, there is a work for some young researcher to examine the vast corpus and reveal the extra-ordinary ability of this man to communicate even during depression.

THIS BOOK

When Mrs Vera Phillips and I were constructing the autobiography of J.B. Phillips that he had left unfinished, we made a habit of reading the day's extract from this book—*Through the Year with J.B. Phillips*—each morning before we started work. Vera, who is now unable to read herself, will still hand the book to any suitable visitor to read the selection of the day. I am glad that it is now being reissued and will be available to a wider range of people. I commend it from experience, knowing how many people have profited from it in the past.

Edwin Robertson

January

To you whom I love I say, let us go on loving one another, for love comes from God. Every man who truly loves is God's son and knows him. But the man who does not love cannot know him at all, for God is love.

1 JOHN 4:7–8

✣

1 January

LOVE IS THE GREATEST

Love is the greatest, for without it, there is no worthwhile success and no real security.

Love is the greatest, for men are never transformed at heart, permanently, except by love.

Love is the greatest for, without it, knowledge can become dangerous and destructive.

Love is the greatest, for it persists beyond the confines of this temporal existence.

Love is the greatest.

✣

2 January

THE POWER OF LOVE

In the New Testament, love means nothing less than the true nature of God. St John assures us that God—the power behind our vast universe—is love, and that the life of his Son Jesus on earth was neither more nor less than the expression of that nature, that love, in terms of human life.

It is an astonishing statement, but it is the very heart of Christianity! The life of Jesus is love.

It is the working out, on a miniature stage, of exactly that quality of person that is the power we call God.

✣

3 January

THE WAY OF LOVE

To change the world, Jesus used love. He set himself to love men and to change them, so that they could share his plans for the building of a worldwide kingdom.

No one shared his temptation in the wilderness so the story of it must have come from his own lips. There he deliberately rejected the methods that have commonly been used to back reform—methods that use material means as a bait, methods that nowadays we should call 'good publicity', indulging in compromise with evil in the hope that good might result.

All these easy and tempting ways he set behind him.

Jesus used the way of love.

He won men's allegiance.

He dared to trust 'the awful slow ways of God'.

These are the ways of love.

✣

4 January

GOD *IS* LOVE

What we need to recover is the conviction that God is not merely kindly disposed towards us, but that he *is* love.

Some theology will not allow us to enjoy this beautiful simplicity. It is far too good to be true! And the implication seems to be that if we were allowed to take John's words at their face value, we should all misbehave ourselves very badly. Consequently we are often told that God's love is not to be imagined in terms of human love, that it is higher, deeper, truer, and sterner.

If we are not very much on our guard, we shall be cheated of the Good News. The inestimable comfort of knowing that God *is* love will be whisked away and we shall be given instead something so poor, unbending and relentless, that, instead of being reassured and inspired, we will be repulsed and frightened.

The Divine Lover will have become 'the Hound of Heaven'.

✣

5 January

WHEN WE LOVE...

If it is true that God *is* love, then it follows that, as John so rightly points out, 'every one that loveth is born of God, and knoweth God'. This we shall find absolutely true to life's experience and to our own.

It is when we love, even a little, that we sense a kinship with the nature of things.

For instance, in the course of true love between a man and a woman, or in the experience of parents with their newborn child—that is, at times of special sensitivity—many ordinary people feel that they are somehow touching reality. Similarly, those who devote their lives wholeheartedly to the service of, shall we say, deaf, blind, or mentally defective children, not infrequently find a satisfying sense that they are in accord with some purpose much greater than themselves.

In the experience of ordinary people, without any particular religious faith, the actions of real love sometimes announce themselves as part of the divine love.

The opposite is equally true. However religious a man may be, however correct his beliefs and punctilious his ritual observances, *unless he loves*, he does not know God.

✣

6 January

THE GREATEST OF THESE...

This new teaching, this new way of living, this living out, in the stuff of everyday life, of the principle of love demanded a new word when Christian literature came to be written. There was no word in the *Koine*, the current Greek *lingua franca* of the time, to express the meaning of the word 'love'. The new word coined had to mean 'being like Christ', expressing him who was love in the ordinary ways of life.

It worked, and slowly men began to translate this great word into their own affairs—so that Paul, from his observation as well as from his conviction, was able to say: 'The greatest of these is love.'

If only we can grasp that it is literally true, that God is not merely loving, but *is* love!

If the great power behind all things is love, then to be linked to that power is really to know life and health and peace.

To be ignorant of love and to live a life shut off from it, means that you cannot know the source of your own being.

He that loveth not, knoweth not God.

'To be saved' or 'to be converted' or 'to be a Christian' is to be at one with the true nature of things; to be at one with love.

✤

7 January

OUR REASONABLE GOD

There is a significant verse in Jude. It says, '*Keep yourselves in the love of God*' (v. 21).

In a sense, we cannot be *beyond* the love of God any more than the prodigal son was really beyond his father's love or out of his father's heart in the far country. But we do not want to waste our lives in far countries, or torture ourselves unnecessarily by making God appear to be our enemy.

In a very real sense, we can keep ourselves in the love of God, not so much by straining after him as by *realizing* him, not merely by avoiding sins, but by *thought, prayer and imagination*; making sure that we are being and doing what at this particular time he wants us to be and do.

God is full of mercy and loving-kindness.

God does not make himself inaccessible to make sport of us poor fumbling mortals.

God is not unreasonable.

✤

8 January

'IN HIM WE LIVE...'

Let us then keep ourselves in the love of God. Tragedy, bereavement, suffering, disappointment, frustration... all these things I observe in the lives of people every week of my life.

Often they cannot be explained. Often a kind of mute sympathy is the most we can offer in the name of the Lord. But how much better if we can somehow, even though it be by a single sentence, suggest that *nothing* is really beyond the power and purpose of God?

However we may be hurt by life, whatever our mistakes and failures, and even though death itself touches us and our loved ones, we can at all times and in all places say triumphantly: *'In him we live and move…'*

⁑

9 January

THE FAILURE OF LOVE

The loss of the sense of God 'in whom we live, and move…' is more often due to *the failure to love* than to any other single cause. And that, since God is by definition Love, is what you might expect.

Sometimes it is a matter of repairing the love and charity in which we hold our neighbours.

Sometimes it is a matter of turning away from obsession with ourselves towards the magnificence of God.

Sometimes it is a matter of quietly absorbing the ceaseless flow of the eternal love.

Sometimes I meet people who have simply cut themselves off from this love of God. Their love has become mere possessiveness or it has become perverted into covetousness, or it has turned in upon itself to become bitter self-pity.

Such people make my heart ache. For, although I would not set any limits to the mercy of God, yet, as far as this life is concerned, it does not look as though, even if they live to be a hundred, they would ever have the sense that 'in him they live and move…'

That makes me very sad.

❖

10 January

THE GOD I WORSHIP

I was not born with my collar turned the wrong way round. In fact, I spent several years disbelieving in any kind of God at all! It took me a lot of hard thinking as well as some experience of life before I found the real God. So I am able to be patient with those who have not yet found their way to a faith which makes sense.

When I did find God (and, of course, I am always finding out more and more about him), I found he was not a bit like the sort of super-father-figure image which has been thrown at me, from various angles, since childhood.

Let me tell you about the God I worship.

Look at the second half of St Matthew, chapter 25, and you will find a picture—the only picture Christ ever gave of the way in which men are going to be judged after this life. It is only a picture, but the truth in that picture stands out vividly.

It is this.

What really matters in God's sight is not how religious a man is, or what his profession is, or how much money he has got, but how he treats other people.

For the sort of God I worship is not only the One who is behind and beyond all creation, but the One who is in us and with us in all the mess and muddle of human life.

I believe this God became a Man.

I believe moreover that *he* laid it down firmly and definitely, that the way in which we treat other people, of either sex, is the way in which we treat him.

✤

11 January

BEHOLD THE MAN!

Honestly admitting the meagre quantity of the records, I want nevertheless to make these three statements.

1. From any intelligent reading of the four Gospels, there arises an impression, strong and living, of someone who is head and shoulders above any other man who ever lived.

2. After translating the Gospels, I find behind these four portraits someone far greater than words could express. Not only then would I recommend the reading of the Gospels, a Gospel at a time if you can, but the use of quiet thought and reverent imagination. These records convey a deep impression of someone who is quite uniquely alive.

3. In spite of the briefness of these Gospel character sketches, we are dealing with Someone who is alive today.

Behold the Man!

There are many people who have found Christ through the fellowship of the Church, but the records of the Bible Society show that the reading of the Scriptures even without the background of Church or Christian fellowship has, in an impressive number of instances, brought men and women into contact with One who has changed the outlook and direction of their lives.

That is surely very remarkable.

✣

12 January

IS THAT NEGATIVE?

Many people look on the Christian religion as a very negative affair, consisting of a lot of 'Thou shalt nots', and certainly including 'Thou shalt not have a good time'!

This is partly the fault of some religious people (who certainly ought to know better), and partly because very few men and women trouble to find out what Jesus himself actually said—and was.

Consider these facts about him:

1. So far from wanting people's lives to be anaemic and negative, Jesus said that he had come to bring them more life than they had ever known before (John 10:10).

2. So far from being a kill-joy and puritan, Jesus enjoyed the good things of life, and even created in the minds of some religious people a reputation for being too fond of good food and the bottle (Luke 7:34).

3. So far from adopting a 'holier-than-thou' attitude, Jesus loved all kinds of people (though he could be shatteringly rude to hypo-crites, religious or otherwise), and thus got a name for keeping bad company (Luke 15:2).

Does all that sound negative?

13 January

'WELCOME HOME!'

I can imagine the prodigal son, making his painful way home, rehearsing again and again his speech of apology, and all the time imagining a furious father. But what really happened? 'While he was yet a great way off, his father… ran, and fell on his neck and kissed him.'

If ever a man had provoked the wrath and indignation of a father, it was surely that prodigal son. Yet the picture of his reception by the father is given to us by Christ himself. It is authentic.

God's attitude of love cannot change.

Men can hurt and punish themselves by defying his laws. They can defraud and impoverish their lives by refusing to accept his love into their hearts. They may even reach a state where his unchanging goodness, love and truth may look to them like a fearful threat (and they may call this the 'wrath' of God). But even in that state they have not 'provoked' him in the human sense.

If we turn to God, we find him as did the prodigal son, his father. It will be: 'Welcome home!'

14 January

HE KNOWS, YOU KNOW

Sometimes we forget how fully human Jesus was. We live on the other side, so to speak, of his triumphant rising from the dead. We did not know him when he trod the hills and streets of Palestine as a mortal man.

We think of Christ as the ascended King in whose hands all power ultimately rests. And we are quite right. But it is a great loss to us if we forget how completely human he really was.

Is life hard and difficult?

Are your burdens too heavy to bear?

Remember that the unseen, but very real God was himself a man once.

He knew temptation.

He knew difficulty.

He knew ingratitude.

He knew disappointment.

He knew the hearts of men, without illusion and without cynicism.

So he understands your heart and mine—fully.

He knows, you know.

✣

15 January

A MATTER OF THE HEART

It has always been the concern of true religion to influence human behaviour. Usually this has meant the growth of a rather complicated set of rules. In the case of the Hebrews, there is no doubt that human behaviour *was* profoundly influenced by such rules.

Nevertheless, among the Hebrew prophets, there came men of spiritual insight who saw more deeply into the problem, and who considered that outward obedience was by no means all that was desirable. They were men who came to proclaim that it was *the inner attitude of the heart* that really mattered, as regards human behaviour *and* in the sight of God.

This great theme was expounded supremely by our Lord Jesus Christ. With his unerring insight, he was able to see deep within us, to see the springs of motive, to see the shams and disguises, to see the boasting and feeble excusing. Steadily he sought to make men aware of their instability of heart, and their need for inner unity.

Jesus taught a religion that started with the heart and with the springs of human action at a time when immense store was set by outward observance.

He taught a religion of changed affections.

Christianity is not merely a set of dogmas.

It is primarily the recovery of a right relationship with God.

That is a matter of the heart.

❖

16 January

THE WHOLE OF LIFE

The Christian religion is concerned with the whole of life.

There have been, and still are, 'religions' which are concerned with the worship of a God or gods, but which have no influence on man's behaviour towards man.

Christianity is not like this. The fact that the Infinite God focused himself in a Man is the best proof that God cares about people.

In the teaching of that Man, Jesus Christ, we find repeated again and again, an insistence on love to God and love to men being inseparably linked. He violently denounced those who divorced religion from life. He had no use at all for those who put up a screen of elaborate ceremonial and long prayers, and exploited their fellow men behind it.

It is a temptation for all of us to separate our love of God from our concern for man. God is all Loveliness and Wonder and Perfection, and our hearts go out towards his great love. But people are imperfect, irritating, stupid and ungrateful, and are not always easy to love. Yet Jesus insisted that the love of God must go hand-in-hand with love of fellow men.

Our relationship with God is intimately bound up with our relationship with our fellow men.

✣

17 January

A CONSTRUCTIVE ATTITUDE

I see no prospect of our even wanting to obey the second commandment—about loving our neighbour—seriously until we have begun to obey the first—about loving God. We do not really see other men and women as our brothers and sisters simply by talking airily about the brotherhood of man. We only see them as such when we begin to get a vision of God the Father.

It is so fatally easy to talk high-falutin hot air about all the world being 'one big family', and yet fail to get on with the members of our own families, or with those who live next door, or in the flat above us. Men do not really love their fellows until they have seriously begun to love God.

It is only then that we learn to drop the destructive attitude of hatred and contempt and criticism, and begin to adopt the constructive attitude of Christian love. So one reason for the command to love God being 'the first and great commandment' is that we do not really keep the second until we have obeyed the first.

✣

18 January

PIONEERS OF THE NEW HUMANITY

Because we are infected by the closed-system mode of thought of our times, we are slow to accept as real and available, the resources of God through his Holy Spirit. We *must* make a determined effort of faith to recapture that New Testament attitude of mind by which God is confidently counted on to provide the necessities for the new life.

We can so easily reflect that 'times were different then', and so excuse ourselves from believing that God is alive and active today. Times *were* different then, but we can be quite certain that, although the enemies and hindrances of the early Church were different from ours, they were certainly no fewer.

The Christian faith took root and flourished in an atmosphere almost entirely pagan, where cruelty and sexual immorality were almost taken for granted, where slavery and the inferiority of women were almost universal, while superstition and rival religions with all kinds of bogus claims existed on every hand. Within this pagan chaos the early Christians, by the power of God within them, lived lives as sons of God, demonstrating purity and honesty, patience and genuine love.

They were pioneers of the new humanity. They lived by the power of God within them.

We must do that too.

Today.

✢

19 January

THE DIMENSION OF GOD

The time is coming when the purely geocentric conception of the human predicament will seem foolish and inadequate. As science discovers more of that unseen which 'programmes' and 'patterns' the seen, it will become more and more clear that physical death is not always a disaster and is never a finality.

Why should it be thought so 'unscientific' to believe in the dimension of God, in spiritual forces and in the spiritual realities which have demonstrable effects upon people?

✣

20 January

TRUE DESTINY

We have come to equate the supernatural with the 'spooky' and the spiritual with the nebulous. But suppose we ourselves are being called to the acceptance of a quite new scale of values. Suppose we are asked to believe that the dimension of ultimate reality is only partially adumbrated by what we see happening in human life? Can we not, on the authority of God's historic visit, make at least a leap of imagination and see our lives as a temporary indication in time and space of something of far greater value and significance?

Must we be so geocentric in our thinking? Can we not see that it is only from *our* point of view that this life looks like the whole?

Could we not for a moment forget to be 'sensible' and 'scientific' and believe that our dreams, our longings and out intuitions, which can never be satisfied in this life, are not vapours of wishful thinking, but quietly insistent reminders of our true destiny?

✣

21 January

WONDER STARTS HERE

The modern acceleration of scientific discovery, the leaps and bounds by which the human mind has progressed in a score of different directions, from agriculture to psychology, are certain, if we use our minds as we should, to expand our conception of God enormously. What is more, this very enlargement of knowledge is enough to show the humble-minded that it is perfectly possible that vista upon vista of unknown Truth has yet to be discovered.

To the man of sensitivity and imagination his own microscopic existence upon this tiny planet, set amid immeasurable whirling universes, seems both precarious and terrifyingly unimportant.

But not if he is a Christian! Not if he believes that the infinite God fitted his stature to our need, and became a human being!

The awe may remain, but once a man accepts with mind and heart that God became Man, the terror and loneliness are gone for ever.

The real wonder starts *there*.

✥

22 January

WHEN ANCHORS SLIP

If it is true that the nature of reality is spiritual and it is only temporarily and incidentally involved in matter, it is not unreasonable to want to know something of the Spiritual Being behind 'the scheme of things'. On those unimaginative people to whom the spiritual has always sounded fanciful and unreal, it is slowly dawning that the physical world which is so real and tangible to them is most uncomfortably unreliable.

A man used to be able to reckon on a good number of years of active material life, which were an efficient buffer between him and the naked spiritual realities which, in his more vulnerable moments, he suspected might be true. Now his buffer of material things has been shown to be far from dependable. At any moment he can be pitch-forked into the world of the spirit.

His anchors are slipping, so, if he feels the need for anchorage (and who, at heart, does not?), he must find it in the world of the spirit.

In other words, he must find God.

23 January

FOUR TRUTHS

There are four fundamental truths which we have got to get across if our Christianity is not to be vague and sentimental. They are the four cardinal doctrines of the Christian Church.

1. *The Incarnation*. The man Jesus did on many occasions claim to be, not merely an inspired teacher, but *the Son of God*. We have got to make up our minds about this claim, one which no other religious leader has ever made. Because of this, what he said and what he was are of the very highest importance to the human race.

2. *The Atonement*. Whereas all religions attempt to bridge the gulf between sinful man and a perfect God, only Christianity succeeds in doing so. The bridge across the chasm was (as it were) built from both sides.

3. *The Resurrection* is a fact of history.

4. *The Holy Spirit*, the Spirit of God, is immediately available to those who call upon him.

These four truths are truths on which we Christians stand.

✤

24 January

THE CHRISTIAN BELIEVES...

The Christian believes in a God of love, all-powerful and all-wise. He believes man to be God's special creation, and whether he believes the fault to derive from the failure of the first man or not, he believes mankind to be suffering from a universal infection called 'sin'.

He is inclined to believe that the non-apprehension of God is chiefly due to this moral infection.

The Christian further believes that the eventual effect of sin is death, and that man would be in a hopeless impasse were it not for God's personal visit to this earth in the man Jesus Christ. This man not only provided a perfect example of human living but by making himself, as it were, representative man, allowed the forces of evil to close in upon him and kill him.

By this action he reconciled the sinful human race with the perfection and holiness of God.

After his death by crucifixion, Jesus returned to life again, both to prove his own claim to be divine, and to demonstrate the fact that he had overcome the power of death.

After his resurrection and ascension, Jesus sent his own Spirit into the personalities of his early followers so that they might be the spearhead of a movement designed to convert the world to belief in, and co-operation with, God himself.

Christians further believe that Jesus Christ founded a Church which is to be, on earth, a witness to heavenly truth, and that he gave that Church unique spiritual authority.

The Church therefore seeks to add to its membership so that men and women may be reconciled with God and may do his will upon earth.

✣

25 January

THE LIFE OF THE AGES

The early Christians had a very strong sense that the 'revealed truth' was very near. Indeed, it might come breaking through at any moment in the personal return of their Lord. Death, which was continually very near them, was not therefore a disaster but simply to step into that wider world—'to depart and be with Christ which is far better'.

It is easy to laugh at the so-called two-storey idea of heaven and earth which is supposed to have been held by the early Christians. But I have become convinced through close study of these Epistles, that it was no crude two-storey idea of heaven and earth which gave the early Church its certainty and vitality. (Indeed, though I am not a historian, I would say that that idea came much later—in the Middle Ages.) No, they appear to me to have grasped, in a way that many of us have not, by the 'faculty of faith' that 'the things which are seen are temporal, but the things which are not seen are eternal'.

They had no technical terms to express this sense of another dimension, but nobody can read the Epistles without feeling the conviction very strongly, that God was the One in whom the Christians 'lived and moved and had their being', and that this temporary and imperfect life of ours is but a tiny part of the 'life of the ages' which God has invited his sons to share.

✟

26 January

ULTIMATE VICTORY

The practical effect of this knowledge of the Real World, separated only by a veil from this mortal life, on the lives of early Christians, was great.

Look at these specific results, for example.

It produced a feeling of special quality about earthly life. Because the very life of God, the heredity of God was in them, they simply could not be conquered whatever might happen to their bodies.

It meant that they were quite certain of the ultimate victory of the purposes of God, despite all the forces of the world and the devil could do. They had before their minds the unforgettable demonstration of power in the raising of Christ from the dead. They confidently reckoned on the same power operating within themselves against the same enemies, a power which was able to carry them through into the world where Christ already reigned.

It meant that they were conscious that, despite all the wear and tear of daily worldly contact, there was a daily renewal from within. The inexhaustible grace of God for them, maintains the inner man.

✥

27 January

A SENSE OF URGENCY

Here are several more effects of that faith the early Christians had about the 'life of the ages':

They believed, literally, that there was a place prepared in heaven for them. Far more certainly than we are sure of a reservation or a booked seat were they sure that they had a building of God 'eternal in the heavens'.

They recognized and accepted the tension that must exist in creatures made for eternity who were living for God's purpose in this infected and limited world. 'In this we groan, being burdened.' By this is meant not so much that they were 'fish out of water', but sons of God who were sometimes groping and fumbling, yet with the certainty that one day they would rise to their full stature, see and know all, and live worthily of their King.

They accepted what we might just as well accept—that 'to be present with the body' meant in a sense 'to be absent from the Lord'.

They felt that the dominating purpose of life is to do the will of God and prove oneself worthy of the high calling. Everything else is to be counted as 'mere rubbish' compared with the prize of winning Christ. So motives and self and profit disappeared.

They considered this life as a period of probation, of training, even a time of 'examination'. They believed that what we do and believe, or fail to do and believe, while we live in these present bodies, would profoundly affect what happened to them when the veil was down and Reality broke through. This gave their lives a sense of urgency and purpose, and greatly deepened their sense of responsibility towards their pagan neighbours.

Nowadays, when we are inclined to imagine that the death of the body almost automatically ushers people into the presence of God (though we feel that, on the whole, the Christians will be rather nearer him than the others), it is salutary to recover this sense of judgment—not judgment in the police-court sense—but judgment by something much more awe-inspiring, judgment by Reality or, as it were, the true nature of God.

✛

28 January

INCREDULOUS

I am incredulous by nature, and as unsuperstitious as they come. I have never bothered about the number thirteen, or walking under ladders (making sure, of course, that there isn't a man with a paint-pot above my head), or any of the many superstitions which may occupy the human heart in the absence of faith. Indeed, I laugh heartily when the predictions of celebrated clairvoyants turn out to be false—as they mostly do.

Anyone can make predictions which are so vague that they are meaningless to any intelligent reader, yet most of the popular press still gives space to 'What the Stars Foretell'.

The late lamented *Picture Post* demonstrated this absurd nonsense of combined astrology and so-called clairvoyance shortly before the Second World War. All the stars, and nearly all the clairvoyants had predicted that there would not be a war. But there was!

I mention this because I am not the sort of person who is readily taken in by the fraud and the plausible liar. Experience as a vicar of a parish soon cures you of this if nothing else will! But from time to time in life, strange things occur which convince me that 'there are more things in heaven and earth than are dreamt of in your philosophy'.

I have had first-hand incontrovertible experience of extra-sensory perception, and a little of precognition.

But the experience I want to mention now is relevant to the matter of the resurrection.

⁜

29 January

'IT'S ALWAYS HAPPENING'

Many of us who believe in what is technically known as the Communion of Saints, must have experienced the sense of nearness, for a fairly short time, of those whom we love soon after they have died. This has certainly happened to me several times. But the late C.S. Lewis, whom I did not know very well, and had only seen in the flesh once, but with whom I had corresponded a fair amount, gave me an unusual experience.

A few days after his death, while I was watching television, he 'appeared' sitting in a chair within a few feet of me, and spoke a few words which were particularly relevant to the difficult circumstances through which I was passing. He was ruddier in complexion than ever, grinning all over his face and, as the old-fashioned saying has it, positively glowing with health.

The interesting thing to me was that I had not been thinking about him at all. I was neither alarmed nor surprised nor did I look up to see the hole in the ceiling that he made on his arrival. He was just there, 'large as life and twice as natural'!

A week later, this time when I was in bed reading before going to sleep, he appeared again, even more rosily radiant than before, and repeated to me the same message, one that was very important to me at the time.

I was a little puzzled by this, and I mentioned it to a certain saintly bishop who was then living in retirement here in Dorset.

His reply was, 'My dear John, this sort of thing is happening all the time.'

✤

30 January

VERIDICAL VISIONS

I mention this personal and memorable experience because although 'Jack Lewis' was real in a certain sense, it did not occur to me that I should reach out and touch him.

It is possible that some of the appearances of the risen Jesus were of this nature, being known technically as 'veridical vision'.

But the writers of the Gospel, in their naïve, unselfconscious way, make it plain that something much more awesome and indeed authoritative characterized Christ's 'infallible proofs'.

✤

31 January

MY CONVICTION

I have known for several years a period of deep darkness which is nowadays known by the technical word 'depression'. It has, incidentally, nothing to do with normal feelings of discouragement and self-pity.

We are often told on television that such states can occur in anyone and that is true. But we are also led to believe that the majority of such sufferers are readily cured through the use of modern anti-depressant drugs, psychiatric treatment, and so on.

This I know to be untrue, not only for me but for quite a proportion of patients who are technically 'depressed'.

In such blackness, all usual appreciation of beauty, love and goodness disappears and with it the sense of a living personal god. *I* would like to state categorically, as I emerge from such a tunnel, that, despite all that my feelings or non-feelings have told me, my convictions remain unshaken.

Who, do you think, is responsible for this?

J.B. Phillips?

Not on your life!

Only the God who is our inescapable contemporary.

✣

We know what love is because Christ laid down his life for us. We must in turn lay down our lives for our brothers. But as for the well-to-do man who sees his brother in want but shuts his heart against him, how could anyone believe that the love of God lives in him? My children, let us love not merely in theory or in words—let us love in sincerity and in practice!

1 JOHN 3:16–18

February

The outward man does indeed suffer wear and tear, but every day the inward man receives fresh strength. These little troubles (which are really so transitory) are winning for us a permanent, glorious and solid reward out of all proportion to our pain. For we are looking all the time not at the visible things but at the invisible. The visible things are transitory: it is the invisible things that are really permanent.

2 CORINTHIANS 4:16–18

✣

1 February

INKLINGS OF ETERNITY

I have *always* been aware of the eternal world. It often seemed to me that I lived in the here-and-now involuntarily and perhaps a little impatiently!

The innumerably clear and sharp experiences of childhood gave me hints and clues to beauty and reality which plainly transcended earthly life. I could not believe that this little life was my permanent home.

The sweetness of music, the loveliness of nature, the beauties of colour and form were, at times, intolerably sweet reminders of some permanent reality lying beyond immediate perception.

Doors opened momentarily but would shut again tantalizingly. But those moments left a fleeting glimpse of unutterable beauty.

At the age of twenty-seven, these inklings of eternity crystallized in a dream or vision so real and so convincing that I can never forget it.

Let me tell you about it.

2 February

THE SEA OF BEING

I had been vaguely ill for some months, and indeed had been forced to resign my first job through ill-health. I lay in hospital, exhausted after a severe and prolonged illness. Physically I was weaker than I had thought it possible for a human being to be and yet remain conscious. I could hear and see, but I could not so much as move a finger nor blink an eyelid by any effort of the will. Yet my mind was perfectly clear, and late one night I overheard a doctor murmur to the night-nurse, 'I am afraid he won't live till the morning.'

In my state of utter exhaustion, this aroused no emotion at all, but I clearly remember making a mental note that patients who are gravely ill and apparently unconscious may yet be able to hear.

I would not say that I felt then the presence of God as a person. I knew him rather as some kind of 'dimension'.

I was, however, a helpless human being resting entirely upon my Creator.

God seemed to be, as it were, the sea of being, supporting me.

I felt that God to be infinitely compassionate and infinitely kind.

✣

3 February

A FIGURE IN WHITE

I fell asleep. Immediately, as it seemed, I had this startlingly vivid dream.

I was alone, depressed and miserable, trudging wearily down a dusty slope. Around me were the wrecks and refuse of human living. There were ruined houses, pools of stagnant water, cast-off shoes, rusty tin cans, worn-out tyres and rubbish of every kind.

Suddenly, as I picked my way through this dreary mess, I looked up. Not far away on the other side of a little valley, was a vista of indescribable beauty. It seemed as though all the loveliness of mountain and stream, of field and forest, of cloud and sky were all displayed with such intensity of beauty that I gasped for breath. The loveliest of scents were wafted across to me. Heart-piercing birdsongs could be clearly heard. The whole vision seemed to promise the answer to my deepest longings as much as does the sight of water to a desperately thirsty man.

I ran towards this glorious world. I knew intuitively that there lay the answer to all my questing, the satisfaction for all that I had most deeply desired. This shining fresh world was the welcoming frontier of my true and permanent home.

I gathered my strength and hurried down the dirty, littered slope.

I noticed that only a tiny stream separated me from all that glory and loveliness. Even as I ran some little part of me realized, with a lifting of the heart, that Bunyan's 'icy river' was, as I had long suspected, only a figment of his imagination. For not only was the stream a very narrow one, but as I approached it, I found that a shining white bridge had been built across it.

I ran towards the bridge, but even as I was about to set foot on it, my heart full of expectant joy, a figure in white appeared before me. He seemed to me supremely gentle but absolutely authoritative. He looked at me smiling, gently shook his head, and pointed me back to the miserable slope down which I had so eagerly run.

I have never known such bitter disappointment, and although I turned obediently, I could not help bursting into tears. This passionate weeping must have awakened me, for the next thing that I remember was the figure of the night-nurse bending over me and saying, rather reproachfully, 'What are you crying for? You've come through tonight—now you're going to live!'

But my heart was too full of the vision for me to make any reply.

What could I say to someone who had not seen what I had seen?

✛

4 February

THE UNFAILING VISION

It is nearly forty years since the night of that dream, but I can only say that it remains as true and as clear to me today as it was then.

Words are almost useless as a means to describe what I saw and felt, even though I have attempted to use them.

I can only record my conviction that I saw reality that night, the bright sparkling fringe of the world that is eternal.

The vision has never faded.

✛

5 February

REVOLUTION

We are inclined to think of the physical world, and even the demonstrable world of the 'ether', as somehow real, while the 'spiritual' is regarded as unreal and imaginary. I believe the opposite to be true. As Paul said long ago: 'the things which are seen are temporal; but the things which are not seen are eternal' (2 Corinthians 4:18).

Suppose what we are seeing and measuring and observing are the outward expressions in the time and space set-up of what is really eternal and spiritual.

If we make such a supposition, we are in for a revolution in our whole way of thinking!

New Testament Christians had already experienced this revolution.

6 February

UNIMAGINED REALITIES

I believe it to be essential for us to recover the dimension of eternity if we are to value this life properly and live it with sanity and courage.

The pieties of former ages cannot satisfy the modern mind. For example, the conception of 'eternity' as merely endless aeons of time, has given many people an idea of 'heaven' which they have rejected as absurd.

Surely here the conception of another 'dimension' can come to the aid of our thought. No thinking Christian today believes in 'heaven' or 'everlasting life' as a mere extension of time-and-space existence, however purified and exalted! He believes that, after the death of the body, there is a release from the time-and-space predicament and a conscious sharing in the timeless Life of God, in which there are probably various stages of enlightenment and knowledge.

There may be no words to describe such a timeless state, but that proves no more than that its reality is beyond present human expression. Yet it remains that unshakeable conviction of Christians, from New Testament days until today, that there is what must be called, for want of a better word, an 'eternal' order, an 'eternal' plan and an 'eternal' life.

Compared with these eternal verities, the present human scene gives no more than a hint of unimagined realities.

✛

7 February

TEMPORARY RESIDENTS

We are only temporary residents here. 'Here we have no continuing city.' Here we can never really be at home. But there, through the incredible love of God, lie breathtaking beauties, unguessable satisfactions, unheard-of delights.

We tend to cling to the small delights of this world, even to try and make them as permanent as we can. But this we can never do, for *we are part of an eternal world.* The things that lift our hearts or catch our breath with wonder or lift us into an ecstasy of delight in the here and now are merely those 'inklings of eternity' to which I referred earlier; echoes of the eternal, changeless world to which, through Christ, we belong.

If we set our hearts on this world or 'lay up treasure' in this world, death will be a bitter wrench. But if we have learned to lay up treasure in heaven, to set our affection on things above rather than on things on the earth, we shall find that there is not one lovely or beautiful thing which we have known here which will not be there, clear and true, permanent and indestructible.

Towards that 'real' world we are all moving.

✤

8 February

THE BACKGROUND OF ETERNITY

It is largely because modern man has lost the sense of what we might call 'the background of eternity' that he sees everything from pleasure to pain in terms of this world only. Yet if he were seriously to accept the attitude of mind which prevails throughout the whole New Testament, he might come to see that, although there are many things which appear to deny the love and justice of God in this life, he is quite literally in no position to judge the final issue.

If he tries to do so, he might easily be as foolish as a man attempting to determine the pattern of a carpet from the examination of a single thread, a picture from a tube of paint, or a book from a box of assorted type.

At most, he is only seeing the raw beginnings of something so enormous as to stagger the imagination.

✣

9 February

NO CONTINUING CITY

Our experiences of love and beauty, much as we may enjoy and appreciate them in this transitory life, are not rooted here at all. We should save ourselves a lot of disillusionment and heartbreak if we remind ourselves constantly that here we have, as I said a little earlier, 'no continuing city'.

The world is rich with all kinds of wonders and beauties, but we only doom ourselves to disappointment if we think that the stuff of this world is permanent. Its change and decay are inevitable.

The rich variety of transitory beauty is no more than a reflection or a foretaste of the real and the permanent.

Something of this thought is surely included in Christ's words: 'lay up for yourselves treasures in heaven, where neither moth nor rust doth corrupt, and where thieves do not break through nor steal' (Matthew 6:20).

✣

10 February

THE CREATOR'S PLAN

It would do us all a power of good if we would take time off, and use our imaginations to see what is really happening on this earth *from the point of view of heaven*. We might then see how pathetically ready man is to be fascinated by what we might call the technical marvels of the age—how thrilled he is with the so-called electronic 'brain', with the breaking of speed records, by the use of artificial satellites, and similar achievements. Yet if we were observing life from the true point of view, we should see how infinitely more important it is to recognize what is really going on in the world of human beings than to goggle at any number of physical marvels.

We should also see how few are trying to find out what the Creator's plan might be for this world, and how even fewer are prepared to co-operate with it.

✢

11 February

EARTHBOUND

The spirit of this age not only refuses to believe that it can be inter-penetrated by another sort of life altogether, but cannot somehow grasp the dimension of eternity at all.

No doubt this is a reaction to the Victorian Christianity which extracted money through the work of the bodies of the ill-housed and then spent a small proportion of the proceeds in building mission halls to save their souls. It is also probably a reaction against the 'pie in the sky' teaching whereby men could absolve themselves from social duties and responsibilities by pointing to the glories that were to come in heaven.

Whatever the causes may be, much of our modern Christianity and almost all of our modern humanism has completely lost the sense of this little life being lived '*sub specie aeternitatis*'. Christianity is therefore often only tolerated because of its social implications. It is very rarely seen as the living out of the life of God in temporary conditions of time and space.

Yet so long as we regard the Christian faith as merely the means of making people behave decently or of reducing the divorce rate or juvenile delinquency, we miss the real beauty and wonder of its quality.

Many Christians seem to me to be utterly earthbound and are very far from realizing that 'here we have no continuing city', that here 'we are strangers and pilgrims', that our true home is in the eternal life of God.

✣

12 February

THE FACULTY OF FAITH

Suppose it is true, as I am sure it is, that we are at all times surrounded and permeated by this 'spiritual' dimension. Suppose, too, that we needed the x-faculty, the faculty of faith, in order to appreciate this further dimension. Can we not see that it is the x-faculty which has deteriorated over the centuries between us and the Church's young days?

I believe we all have this faculty, but that, in most of us, it has become atrophied almost to vanishing point. Now, since it is obvious throughout the New Testament that the x-faculty is the indispensable link between the resources of the unseen world and this temporary one, we can easily understand how the serious falling off in the use and practice of 'faith' throughout the Church at large has resulted in a marked loss of spiritual power.

Yet it would appear that one of the great reasons for our living on this planet at all is that we may learn to use and develop this faculty.

If we do not use our faith-faculty, we are bound to be out of harmony with the divine plan.

Why this should be so we simply do not know, but it is one of the primary facts that we have to accept.

✣

13 February

'HAVE FAITH IN GOD!'

Jesus' observation of the failure of men to use their faculty of faith must have continually astonished him. To him the unseen dimension and order were continually real. The love, the generosity, and the power of the Father were constant realities, and it must not only have amazed him but also grieved him more than we can guess to find men either unwilling or unable to use the power of faith.

Again and again he urges men to 'have faith in God'; and both by his own teaching and his own example, it is plain that he is continually urging men to put the weight of their confidence, not in earthly schemes and values, but in the unseen 'heavenly order', of which the supreme Head is the Father.

To live like this, to live as though the spiritual realities were infinitely more important than the appearance of things, might fairly be said to be a basic teaching of Jesus.

✛

14 February

THE ETERNAL ORDER

The heroes of Old Testament days were invariably the men, and in some cases the women, who exercised their faculty of faith *even when it appeared to contradict the evidence of their five senses*. In those old days, the king, the prophet, the priest, the warrior, sensed intuitively what has today become very largely a missing dimension.

There is much in the Old Testament which may strike us as outmoded and even tedious, but its particular genius is to point to and record the actions of these people who were, however dimly, living with a consciousness of the eternal order.

When we come to the pages of the New Testament, we find this faculty vastly enhanced.

15 February

A CLOSED SYSTEM

The mental climate of our age affects us all, whether Christians or not, far more than we know. We have become conditioned to regard this earthly life of ours as a completely closed system of cause and effect.

Because science has made such enormous strides, and can explain to our satisfaction so much of the physical world, and can offer intelligent explanations of what was previously sheer mystery, we are inclined to forget that science at its apparently most omniscient *is only dealing with one particular stratum or aspect of truth*.

Again, modern psychology has made enormous strides in the understanding and explanation of human behaviour. But while it throws a great deal of light on what was previously dark (and has, we hope, more light to shed), we need to remember that *the psychologist also is dealing only with certain aspects of truth*—in this case emotional and mental life.

We should be foolish to disregard this new knowledge, but we should be still more foolish if we thought that, by means of physical and mental science, the whole of life can now be accounted for. It seems to me that we are missing out a dimension in our thinking which we may call for the moment the dimension of God.

It was awareness of this dimension which produced the startling vigour and unassailable certainty of the young Church.

✤

16 February

WRONG TOOLS

God is not discoverable or demonstrable by purely scientific means, unfortunately for the scientifically-minded.

But that really proves nothing.

It simply means that the wrong instruments are being used for the job.

❖

17 February

NO SUNSET TOUCH

A view of life which at once accepts man's present limitations and believes in his ultimate potentialities, is only possible to the one who has true religious faith. The man who has no religion, and denies the possibility of there being any such thing, imprisons himself within the closed-system of physical life upon this planet.

This is the position of the agnostic who, according to the Oxford dictionary definition is 'one who holds that nothing is known, or likely to be known of the existence of a God or of anything beyond material phenomena'. The dreams of the poet, the visions of the artist, the 'pattern' apprehended by the truly religious man, have all to be explained as purely subjective phenomena within the material set-up. All the hopes, joys, inklings and intuitions which seem to have a point of reference outside the physical world must be shown up for the illusion that they are. Every 'intimation of immortality', every 'sunset touch', every sense of awe and wonder and mystery have to be seen through and explained away.

For the true agnostic, the material dimension is the only dimension.

There is no reality beyond this reality, no purpose and no God.

✢

18 February

NON-SCIENTIFIC WAYS

Poets, artists of every kind, mystics and indeed ordinary people of faith may be receiving truth in an entirely different way from that to which the scientist is accustomed. It is not in the least that his own wholly admirable and painstaking methods are being ignored or, so to speak, short-circuited. It is simply that there are ways of apprehending some kinds of truth which are quite independent of this scientific method.

Sometimes these are intuitive and sometimes they are developed by long practice. Sometimes they are both.

I think the honest scientist cannot help admitting this. Perhaps therefore he may be persuaded to see what I myself find quite plain— that the more man's attention is concentrated upon the material, the more his spiritual faculties become atrophied.

✢

19 February

THROUGH ANOTHER DOOR

Our certainty is not to be certainty based on external authority, but it is an inward conviction through the faculty of faith. This faculty which, to me, is so important, is as real as the faculty of hearing or of sight or of intellectual activities such as calculation or discrimination.

'Faith' does sometimes mean continuing to hold on to what we believe to be true in the face of apparent contradiction, darkness and so on. But here I am talking of *faith* as the God-implanted faculty that enables us to grasp his truth.

There is something in us that recognizes the truth of God. It is not a scientific truth. It is not a historic truth. It is not even a psycho-logical truth. It is truth entering by another door altogether, speaking as it were almost another language.

It is the Word of eternal life and it carries its own inherent quality.

In other words, it is the voice of the 'real world' speaking to us and it is recognized by us, even while we are living in this temporary dimension that we call life.

✥

20 February

EARTHLY RELIGION

Although Christianity leads to human thought and aspirations far beyond the limitations of this present stage of existence, and is thus in a sense an other-worldly religion, it is also incurably earthly. Men may have their visions, but they are required to work them out in the everyday stuff of human situations.

There is no room for mystical escapism. We find God-become-man himself involved in the messes and miseries of the human situation and requiring his followers to do the same.

A man whose life is united with the timeless life of God through sincere and intelligent faith in Christ becomes strongly aware of his eternal destiny, and all kinds of inexpressible hopes for the distant future begin to stir in his mind. But he has to learn and to act in this present world, accepting good-humouredly his physical limitations and a fair degree of spiritual blindness.

He has to express what is spiritually true in the context of ordinary human relationships and ordinary human problems.

✤

21 February

THE RING OF TRUTH

I suppose I must have read as many myths as most men, both in Latin and Greek as well as, in translation, in other European and Asiatic languages. They can be helpful. Even now we can 'get the message' of the Sirens of Circe about whom Homer wrote nearly three thousand years ago. But, apart from the Book of Revelation, which stands in a class by itself, the New Testament is not myth. Its sparse vocabulary, its lack of writing for effect, its general atmosphere of understatement is miles removed from the fantastic world of magic and myth.

Here in the dark, cruel, fear-ridden world of what we now call the first century, there came to birth in such unlikely places as Corinth and Ephesus, a new kind of human being and human community. Perhaps I was fortunate in starting, not in some 'quest for the historical Jesus', but in the most intimate imaginative contact with the letters of Paul.

For here I found real people, real situations, real victories, and a few real failures.

Here is irrefutable evidence, that long before any 'Gospel' was written, people were being fundamentally changed in character and outlook. This new unquenchable courage and certainty about God was never dreamed up.

The more closely I studied, the more I felt the hallmark of reality and the ring of truth.

✛

22 February

STILL HERE

People sometimes write to me and ask if I believe that the Bible is inspired. If a book can change people, change their whole outlook and give them fresh hope and peace of mind, then I reckon that book is inspired.

When I say you have got to go back about 2,000 years to read the inspired records of what sort of person Jesus really was and how Christianity began, I do not mean you have to stay there. We have to live in a world which is very different in all sorts of ways. But nevertheless the fundamental problems are still the same. We have still got to learn how to love and understand one another. We have still got to learn how to control our human impulses. We still need to be told that we are loved and accepted by God, that our real security lies not in money in the bank, but in the living God. We need to recapture the shining certainty of the early Christians for whom this life was only a preparation for something much more important.

We will not be so troubled by the tensions and pressures of this modern world if our roots are firmly fixed in God. For, although I think our ideas of him have widened and deepened, God has not changed with the passing centuries. He is still there for the man who turns to him.

Or, to put it another way entirely, he is still here to strengthen and support us once we have invited him to enter our personalities.

✤

23 February

PREJUDICED

Prejudiced? Of course I am prejudiced. Every one of us is, but at least, if we are adult and educated, we can be aware of our bias and make proper adjustment. I can only say that in translating the Greek of the New Testament into modern English I made every effort to correct any bias of which I was conscious.

When I came to compare it with the writings which were excluded from the New Testament by the early 'Fathers', I can only admire their wisdom. Probably most people have not had the opportunity to read the apocryphal 'gospels' and 'epistles', although every scholar has. I can only say here that in such writings we live in a world of magic and make-believe, of myth and fancy.

In the whole task of translating the New Testament, I never for one moment, however provoked and challenged I might be, felt that I was being swept away into a world of spookiness, witchcraft and magical powers such as abound in the books rejected from the New Testament.

It was the sustained down-to-earth faith of the New Testament writers which conveyed to me that inexpressible sense of the genuine and the authentic.

✤

24 February

INSPIRED

The New Testament, given a fair hearing, does not need me or anyone else to defend it. It has the proper ring for anyone who has not lost his ear for truth. But because, in these days, it has been compromised in the eyes of many people by those who should know better, I feel I can do no other than record my own impressions as honestly and faithfully as I can.

As the years have passed—and it is now many, many years since I began translating the 'Epistles'—my conviction has grown that the New Testament is, in a quite special sense, *inspired*. It is not magical, nor is it faultless. Human beings wrote it. But by something which I would not hesitate to describe as a miracle, there is a concentration upon that area of inner truth in it which is fundamental and ageless.

That, I believe, is the reason why millions of people have heard the voice of God speaking to them through these amazing pages.

❖

25 February

A MINOR MIRACLE

In translating the Gospels, like every other conscientious modern translator, I emptied my mind as far as possible of preconceived ideas and conclusions. 'Here,' I said to myself in effect, 'are four pieces of Greek, comparatively simple Greek, which it is my job to turn into the sort of English which is spoken and written today.'

I did my best to be detached and disinterested, for it is no part of a translator's job to add colour or give a slant to what he is translating. Yet I find, on comparing notes with other translators, that I am not alone in finding a minor miracle happening.

As the work went on, steadily and inexorably, there stood up from these pages a figure of far more than human stature and quality.

✤

26 February

NO MYTH

The four Gospels are not biographies in the modern sense. I sometimes wish they were! What biographer of a great man today would
omit all references to his subject's home-life, the influence of his
friends, his development during adolescence and his early manhood,
and fail to give any description of his personal appearance?

No one writing today would miss out so many details of times and
places, so that if we take the combined evidence of Matthew, Mark,
Luke and John, we still do not know how long the ministry of Jesus
lasted.

We can find several apparent contradictions. For example, was most
of Jesus' ministry confined to Jerusalem, as John suggests, or was his
work mostly done in the little towns and villages outside?

Of one thing we can be quite certain. The four evangelists never
got together round a table and agreed on the story they would tell!

If we approach the evidence of the Gospels as though they were
written down as evidence for the police, or even as a story for a newspaper, we are bound to be baffled and disappointed. But of course
they were not written in that way at all. The earliest of them, Mark's,
was probably written in AD65 and the latest, John's, about AD90.

It is easy for the enemies of the Christian faith to decry the value
of the four Gospels, and to say that, as history, they have little worth.
These, say the critics, are 'myths', the folklore of the day, and can be
dismissed. They may be based upon some historical events, but at
this stage it is impossible to disentangle fact from fancy.

I write as one who has studied the New Testament very closely for
many years, and I do not believe there is any truth at all in this 'myth'
idea. A 'myth' is a fanciful tale, a fairy-story.

But there is no flavour of myth in the Gospels.

27 February

A STRANGE ATTRACTIVENESS

To study the Gospels closely and, what is even better, to read them right through at a sitting, leaves one with a tremendous impression of a personality who is really far too big for the pen of man to describe.

I don't think it is only because I am a Christian already that a living person forms itself in the mind and touches both heart and imagination.

If the Christian faith is right, this is only what one would expect. But I think it worth recording that, even when I deliberately made the attempt to empty my mind of preconceived ideas and translate the Greek of that day into the English of this day, the sheer force of Christ's strange attractiveness kept breaking through.

✣

28 February

THE LIVELY WORD

It may be that, in the providence of God, it is better that all the books that could have been written (of which St John speaks so airily—John 21:25) were not written. We can see, in the Acts of the Apostles, how the living Spirit of God led and even drove people to cope with their contemporary situation. If we had a full biography of Christ in the modern sense of the word, we might very easily move our emphasis back into the past to the time and place where God became Man, and fail to respond to the winds and pressures of his gentle but insistent Spirit today.

Let us be grateful then to Matthew, Mark, Luke and John for their partial sketches which our reverent thought and imagination can fill in for us. But let us never forget the actual promises made by our Lord.

Not only is he with us always, not only does he promise his Spirit to lead us into the true and right way to deal with any situation, but he also guarantees that, by his Spirit, he will live within our own spirits, producing in us, if we will let him, the Son of God quality which he himself so perfectly exhibited.

The records are 'the Word of God'. But it is *the Living Word* that matters, the Jesus Christ, whom we worship and adore today and by whose power alone, we cope victoriously with all that life may bring.

A lively Word, indeed.

✣

29 February

THE GREAT REALITY

There is an electric 'liveness' about the New Testament. As you work with it, you do your best to be detached. You say to yourself, 'This is just a piece of rather simple first century Greek.' But it isn't! It stings, comforts, challenges and speaks to *you*.

There is no way of hiding from what it has to say about God and man. Even its apparent simplicity, even its strange omissions and reticences, even its occasional repetitions do not alter the overall effect.

In the world of the New Testament, we are plunged into an atmosphere, not of speculation but of certainty.

Men and women *know* that God 'has visited and redeemed his people'.

God is the great reality.

His resources are available and endless.

His promises are real and glorious, beyond our wildest dreams.

❖

We know, for instance, that if our earthly dwelling were taken down, like a tent, we have a permanent house in heaven, made, not by man, but by God. In this present frame we sigh with deep longing for our heavenly house, for we do not want to face utter nakedness. So long as we are clothed in this temporary dwelling we have a painful longing, not because we want just to get rid of these 'clothes', but because we want to know the full cover of the permanent. We want our transitory life to be absorbed into the life that is eternal.

2 CORINTHIANS 5:1–4

March

When all kinds of trials and temptations crowd into your lives, my brothers, don't resent them as intruders, but welcome them as friends! Realize that they come to test your faith and to produce in you the quality of endurance. But let the process go on until that endurance is fully developed, and you will find you have become men of mature character, men of integrity with no weak spots. And if, in the process, any of you does not know how to meet any particular problem he has only to ask God—who gives generously to all men without making them feel guilty—and he may be quite sure that the necessary wisdom will be given him.

JAMES 1:2–5

✣

1 March

ARROGANCE?

Jesus gave three remarkable indications by which men could know (not by scientific 'proof', but by an inward conviction that is perfectly valid to him in whom it arises) that his claim and his revelation are true. They are contained in three sayings of his which are well known to anyone even moderately familiar with the Gospels.

They are:

1. If any man will do his (that is, God's) will, he shall know of the doctrine, whether it be of God or whether I speak of myself (John 7:17).
2. He that hath seen me hath seen the Father (John 14:9).

3. I am the way, the truth, and the life: no man cometh unto the Father, but by me (John 14:6).

These three sayings, especially the last two, are intolerably arrogant if they come from a purely human moral teacher, but they must inevitably be said by Jesus Christ if he is really God.

❖

2 March

TO DO IS TO KNOW

Let us consider the significance of the three sayings I quoted yesterday.

1. Jesus says, in effect, that there will be no inward endorsement of the truth of the way of living he puts forward as the right one until a man is prepared to do the will, that is, co-operate with the purpose, of God. This at once rules out armchair critics of Christianity and any dilettante appraisal of its merits. 'You can't know,' says Christ, 'until you are willing to do.'

2. Christ unquestionably claims to present accurately and authentically the Character of God. As we have seen above, he cannot present the *whole* of God, but he can present in human form a Character that may be understood, admired, loved, respected—or even feared and hated.

3. If Jesus Christ was God, he *must* say that he is the way, the truth and the life, or words of equivalent meaning. We find he adds, as a matter of unalterable fact, that no one comes into contact with God except through him.

✜

3 March

UNIQUE CHARACTER

The flashes of light on this character which the four Gospels reveal are often surprising.

Jesus was not some penniless ascetic like John the Baptist before him. Luke records that there were many women who 'ministered to him of their substance'.

We may be pretty sure that the house of Mary and Martha was not the only home where he could find rest and refreshment. His cloak, 'woven without seam', was hardly the covering of a beggar.

There can be no doubt that he was socially popular, and, although we can discount the jibe that he was a 'gluttonous man and a wine-bibber', we can fairly infer that he enjoyed God's good gifts of food and wine.

It has struck me again and again that some of the unexpected sayings and actions of Jesus were recorded just because they were unexpected. The routine work (if we might so describe it) is sometimes dismissed in a few words—'he went about doing good and healing all manner of sickness and disease among the people'. But the other words and works, which no one could have anticipated and which must have been nearly inexplicable at the time, are treasured and remembered with the utmost fidelity.

✜

4 March

NO EASY WAY

The Christian way of living is not easy. We may have unfortunate temperaments or we may be full of fears and anxieties—and there is nothing like fear for preventing us from really loving other people. The

Christian answer to this is that God is 'willing and able' to change you and strengthen you inside your personality.

You may not believe that at this moment, but millions have proved that God is living, active, contemporary and available. The real, deep, basic reason why I believe the Christian faith to be true is the change that it can make in people.

Or rather, that Christ can make.

5 March

THE LIVING CHRIST

If Jesus Christ never lived or died or rose again, how do you account for the fact that, about AD54, that is ten years before any of the Gospels were written, men and women were being changed in a place like Corinth, a byword even in those days for immorality? Thieves, rogues, prostitutes, perverts, racketeers—all were being changed into honest men and women.

It isn't only these early Corinthians who impress me. It is the people with whom *I* come into contact, or who write to me. Some are young, some middle-aged, some old. They come from places as far away as Australia, Chicago, India. *All* tell me the same story. Christ has become to them a living Person, their strength and companion, the transforming influence in their lives.

I find that very impressive.

6 March

CHANGED LIVES

I had a letter from a young man at Oxford who attributed his conversion to Christianity to reading through my *Letters to the Young*

Churches. I have, through the years, had an almost unceasing flow of correspondence from people, young and old, from all over the English-speaking world, who have told me that God spoke to them through my translation.

I was, and am, overwhelmed by the success of my efforts, but I am not stupid enough to claim the credit for the changed lives and the enlightened understandings.

It is God's work.

The most I have done is remove obscurity and allow the truth to be comprehended.

✛

7 March

LIVING DANGEROUSLY

Luke's story of the young Church in action bears the same stamp of supra-human quality that we find in the Gospels.

The sick are not merely prayed about. They are healed, often suddenly and dramatically.

Mental and psychological diseases ('possession by evil spirits', in the jargon of those days) proved equally susceptible to the new power in the Church.

Perhaps, above all, that miracle which is theoretically unattainable is performed again and again—human nature is changed.

The fresh air of heaven blows gustily through these pages, and the sense that ordinary human life is continually open to the Spirit of God is very marked.

There is not yet a dead hand of tradition. There is no over-organization to stifle initiative. There is neither security nor complacency to destroy sensitivity to the living God.

The early Church lived dangerously.

8 March

WAY OF LIFE

If I thought that the Christian faith was only concerned with church-going or looking after a pious minority, I should have very little use for it. But it isn't. Christianity is concerned with the whole of life, from falling in love to the way you bring up your children, from the use you make of your money or talents to the way you treat your neighbour, from the mystery of birth to the mystery of death and with everything that happens in between.

The Christian faith was a way of life before it became a religion. It still is. You cannot take a certain proportion of life and call that 'religious', any more than you can give God an hour or two on Sunday and consider the rest of life your own. The way you live, the way you treat others—these are the important things, whether you profess to be a believer or not.

For the way in which we behave is an accurate indication of what we really think about God.

If you don't believe me, look at the closing verses of Matthew's Gospel, chapter 25 again.

9 March

BIG GOD

I once asked a group of young people in a London youth group to answer quickly, without thinking too much, the following question: 'Do you think God understands radar?' Several of them said 'No', and then laughed as they realized what they were saying. But that quick answer confirmed what I suspected, namely that, in many of their minds, there lurked an idea of God as the 'Old Gentleman in the sky', somewhat old-fashioned and a little bewildered by modern progress.

We can help young people enormously if we can show them, as they grow, a growing idea of the greatness of God.

I sometimes think the churches are themselves partly to blame because of some of their stained-glass windows and religious pictures. We need to give, in this scientific age, *an idea of God that is big and wide and high*.

Science, which many almost worship, is really only rediscovering the thoughts of God.

It would do good if in Bibles and prayer books, we not only had little religious pictures but also photographs of such things as the spiral nebulae and the Milky Way!

✣

10 March

THE KNOWN GOD

The Greeks had a word for it! But they were a bit baffled when it came to the mysterious power behind the universe, whom some people call 'God'. They had their gods all right, plenty of them—the god of love, the god of hunting, the god of food, the god of drink, the god of luck, and all the rest! But *the* God, the One behind all *love* and truth and beauty, behind the whole complex 'scheme of life', they could only call 'the God whom nobody knows'.

They once put up an altar to him under that title (Acts 17:23).

Many people today feel rather like the Greeks did then. They perhaps had an idea of God when they were children, but that does not satisfy them now. Life is so big and complicated and difficult that the little ideas of God they may have had years ago, are not somehow big enough to fit in with their adult experience. So although they would not call themselves atheists, for them God remains the Great Unknowable, the Mystery that no man can hope to understand.

But God, the great unfathomable Mystery, chose to make himself known to human beings by actually becoming a human being himself, so that people could see what sort of character he has and what sort of meaning and purpose life contains.

In other words, if God wanted men to understand him, he had to come to their level and speak their language.

This is what he did.

In Jesus.

÷

11 March

TOO SMALL

The trouble with many people today is that they have not found a God big enough for modern needs. While their experience of life has grown in a score of directions, and their mental horizons have been expanded to the point of bewilderment by world events and by scientific discoveries, their ideas of God have remained largely static.

It is obviously impossible for an adult to worship the conception of God that exists in the mind of a child of Sunday school age, unless he is prepared to deny his own experience of life. If, by a great effort of will, he does do this, he will always be secretly afraid lest some new truth may expose the juvenility of his faith.

It will always be by such an effort that he either worships or serves a God who is really too small to command his adult loyalty and co-operation.

12 March

THE GRAND OLD MAN

There is much in our churches and religious teaching generally that tends to encourage the 'old-fashioned' concept of God as a 'Grand Old Man' image.

The Bible is often read in beautiful but old-fashioned language.

Our services are often conducted wholly in a form of language that no one uses today.

Many still address God in their prayers in the archaic second person singular—and these prayers themselves often give the impression of being cast in a form that the Grand Old Man can both understand and approve.

Our hymns, with some notable exceptions, often express a Victorian and very rarely a 'big enough' idea of God. To appreciate their true value they should be read aloud in cold blood and dissociated from the well-loved tunes.

At baptism, matrimony, and burial, we continue to use language which ordinary people can hardly understand, but which they feel vaguely is old-fashioned and out of touch with their actual lives. People respect the Grand Old Man and his peculiarities, but they feel no inclination to worship him as the living God.

Why do we deny, by our actions, that God is our contemporary?

✣

13 March

THE RESOURCES OF GOD

The time has come for the Church to restate boldly and unequivocally that the way, the truth and the life have all been revealed, that the

Kingdom is here already and that the battle in which there can be no neutrality is on.

The bankruptcy of humanism *without God* should be ruthlessly exposed and its disquieting similarity to godless Communism deliberately pointed out. The added depth, the added dimension, which human life receives when linked to the timeless Life of God, should be fearlessly proclaimed.

False gods do not exhibit their power or even their existence until the living God is experienced. Sin and failure have no meaning until the challenge of a new way of living is thrown down.

Non-committal agnosticism is never seen as an avoidance of the responsibility of living so long as the truth remains unknown.

No man knows the strength of the enemy until he has fully enlisted on one side or the other.

People will never take evil seriously nor even see much need to tap the resources of God until they join in with the costly redemptive purposes of love.

✢

14 March

WHAT A WASTE

From the angels' point of view, what enormous waste of energy, courage, talent, and personality there must be in many of man's highly lauded projects. The angels might well ask themselves, 'Why does he want to go so fast, to climb so high, to dive so deep, and to complicate his life with so many inventions while he leaves the heart of the matter untouched?' For since man has been promised a share in the timeless life of God, how blind and earthbound he must appear as he spends his best ingenuities, his highest intellects, and the bulk of his resources upon what is merely ephemeral!

If a thousandth part of the devotion and energy which are so freely given to athletic achievement or scientific research were devoted to the building of the Kingdom of God, to better understanding between people, to the production of a true brotherhood between nations, what vast forward strides man, as a potential son of God, could make.

But, alas, he can plainly be seen by the angels to be, consciously or unconsciously, avoiding the real issues, where the personal cost is likely to be high.

✣

15 March

INESCAPABLE

Shafts of divine light, of truths not discoverable by 'scientific' means, have broken through upon the human scene through poets, philosophers and sages, as well as through the founders of various religions.

This fact no intelligent modern Christian would minimize, but such fragments of revelation can, he believes, be only secondary to the planned personal focusing of God in the man Jesus Christ. Indeed the more seriously he takes his own faith, the less it seems to him that the overwhelming significance of that event has so far been rightly appreciated.

If, as the Christian believes, God has actually entered the human scene, then there is an inescapable uniqueness about Christianity. If this is 'the real thing', then, in a sense, there can be no compromise with anything less.

This does not mean lack of sympathy with other religions, but it does mean there is a determination on our part that all men shall know the fullest possible truth.

❖

16 March

PEACE

As we study New Testament Christianity, we are aware that there is an inner core of tranquillity and stability. It fact, not the least of the impressive qualities which the Church could demonstrate to the pagan world was this ballast of inward peace. It was, I think, something new that was appearing in the lives of human beings.

It was not mere absence of strife or conflict, and certainly not the absence of what ordinarily makes for anxiety. Neither was it a lack of sensitivity nor a complacent self-satisfaction, which can often produce an apparent tranquillity of spirit. It was a positive peace, a solid foundation which held fast amid all the turmoil of human experience.

It was, in short, the experience of Christ's bequest when he said, 'Peace I leave with you, my peace I give unto you: not as the world giveth, give I unto you.'

❖

17 March

QUIET

There are some essentials for the maintenance of real Christian living.

The first essential need is for quiet. The higher the function of the human spirit, the more the necessity for quietness.

We cannot, for example, solve a difficult mathematical problem, neither can we appreciate good music, nor indeed art in any form, if we are surrounded by noisy distractions.

It is imperative that, somehow or other, we make for ourselves a period of quiet each day.

If we see the absolute need for this period of quiet, our ingenuity will find a way of securing it.

18 March

THE SPACE WE NEED

We need that quiet space in our lives. It is absolutely essential. Nothing is more important than securing this space amid all our busyness. No one is too busy to set aside a period of, say, a quarter of an hour each day for such quiet.

We are all rather ridiculous here. For if we knew for certain that a space of a quarter of an hour's quiet was essential for our physical health, we should unhesitatingly make room for it. It would become a top priority. Can we not see that such a period, which should be regarded as a minimum, could be absolutely essential for our spiritual health?

For many people this period of quiet must of necessity be solitary, but since a great deal of the vigour of the early Church depended on Christian fellowship and was, in fact, given and demonstrated through Christian fellowship, there is good reason to suppose that a small God-seeking group of people might help one another enormously in redeveloping the faith-faculty.

19 March

THE BUSY CHRISTIAN

The Christian who is spiritually linked to the timeless life of God, and is, not by courtesy title but in reality, a son of God, cannot escape a certain painful tension throughout his earthly life. He is only a temporary resident here. His home, his treasure, the final fulfilment of his hope, does not lie in this transitory life at all.

He must resist the temptation to withdraw from this benighted, sin-infected world, and spend all his spare time in pietistic reflection on the world to which he is bound.

He must hold fast to the belief that God is active and contemporary, working wherever he is given opportunity, in the present passing scene.

'My Father is busy up to this very moment,' said Christ, 'and so am I.'

The servant is in the same position as his Master.

He too must be busy as his Father is busy.

✣

20 March

RECIPE FOR HAPPINESS

There is a right way to do everything—and usually dozens of wrong ones. If you have been muddling along, doing a job in any old way, what a relief it is to be shown by an expert how the thing really should be done. Not only do we save ourselves much wear and tear, but we feel much more satisfied when we have learned the right way, even though it may hurt our pride a bit to unlearn the method we were using.

Christians believe that there is a right way of doing the most important job of all—living, and there are plenty of wrong ones. They believe that Jesus Christ, who claimed to be God living on this earth as Man, gave us the clue to the right way of living—what we might call the recipe for happiness.

This recipe comes in what is often called the Sermon on the Mount, in St Matthew's Gospel (chapter 5, verses 3–11).

It is a pretty revolutionary recipe.

✣

21 March

THE END OF ESTRANGEMENT

I always hesitate to use the word 'sin' simply because it almost always means that people think of some particular sin or sins. When I use it now, I am using it deliberately to describe that which produces and underlines our estrangement from God. Our difference from God is not one of intelligence, or even of size or degree, but a difference in *quality*. He is good, and we, by our sins and those of the race to which we belong, have created the gulf between us and the love of the Father.

We may know that the love of the Father is unalterable love and unconditional love, but our moral failure, not our intellectual stupidity is the basis of our estrangement.

But if, as St Paul asks, good behaviour could bridge the moral gulf, why the bitter necessity of the shame and degradation of the cross? The fact is that we have to drop our excuses and our pretences, our ingenuities and our attempts at self-justification and accept an act of unbelievable humility which we never planned.

When we do this, when we accept, by our 'faculty of faith', this awe-inspiring Act of Reconciliation, we are right with God.

There is now nothing at all between us and the wonder of the love of God.

✣

22 March

PULL-BACK

As in every evolutionary process, including the growth of a normal human being, there is a force which pulls upwards. But there is also a force making for relapse and regression.

We must not be surprised to find a man whose eyes have been opened to spiritual reality experiencing, again and again, reactionary forces within himself. He is, I believe, being drawn to a higher level of human living, a greater awareness, and a greater responsibility. But, in the nature of things, there will inevitably be a pull-back to the former, more comfortable, mode of non-committed thinking and feeling.

❖

23 March

WHEN THE ATTACK BEGINS

It appears to me, comparing my own experience with that of many friends, that once one has seriously enlisted on the side of God and his purpose, considerable spiritual opposition is provoked and encountered. Pull-back is real! Quite apart from one's own tendency to regress and quite apart from the atmosphere of non-faith in which many Christians have to live, the Christian finds himself attacked by nameless spiritual forces.

It is very easy for the non-committed agnostic, or indeed for any non-Christian to make light of an organized force of evil. But it is highly significant to me to find that, in every case of a person becoming a Christian of which I have personal knowledge, this sense of spiritual opposition is experienced, and sometimes felt very keenly.

If we may personify the forces of evil for a moment, it would appear that 'Satan' does not bother to attack, for example, a university professor of philosophy, a popular film star, a busy farmer, a telephone operator or a worker in heavy industry, or anyone else, as long as they are uncommitted in the real spiritual battle. There is no particular point in producing pressures of evil against a man or woman who moves harmlessly and respectably with the normal currents of contemporary human living. But should they once begin to embark on real living and to assist in the building of the Kingdom of God, *then* the attack begins!

✣

24 March

HE SUFFERS TOO

I believe in a God of love, but there are plenty of things which appear to contradict this. I have seen many tragic happenings in my life and I do not see any easy explanation of them. Even nature can at one time seem to be full of 'all things bright and beautiful' and at another 'red in tooth and claw'.

Although I do not claim to know the complete answer to all these contradictions, I have found clues which have helped me along the way. The chief of these is that I have come to see that the vast unknowable power behind the universe, and any other universe too, became one of us in the Man Jesus Christ.

If people tell you that 'all religions are the same', it simply displays their ignorance. No other religion comes within miles of suggesting that the unknowable God became known in a Man, that he suffered pain, disgrace and finally a criminal's death, and that he then rose again to show that death also was conquered. And that is not all. Jesus Christ taught that he is with us in the here and now, with us in all our trials and difficulties, and promises us a place in the next stage of existence which lies beyond time and space.

This means that when I meet suffering, as I often do, I can truly believe that God is in that suffering, and is trying to transform it to fit his ultimate purpose for mankind.

That is, it seems to me, another revolutionary thought.

❖

PASSION

'Passion' is a word whose meaning has changed over the centuries. Today we use it mainly to describe a fit of bad temper or the deep feelings aroused by romantic love. But originally passion came from the Latin word *passio*, which means 'suffering'.

When the churches speak of the Passion of Christ, they are speaking quite simply of his *suffering* for mankind. The God whom Christians worship is a God intimately connected with human beings, their sorrows and their sins. The symbol of the faith is a cross of suffering.

We should all like life to be free from suffering, and our love to be free from pain. But there is no true love without suffering. So the highest love of all, the love of Christ for men, showed unforgettably how deeply he must suffer in order to bring men to himself.

'God was in Christ, reconciling men to himself' wrote St Paul. There, compressed in a few highly charged words, is the heart of the Good News.

We have a God who loves.

That means that we have a God who suffers.

26 March

THE GATEWAY

Without faith in Christ, the most we have is a wistful hope. But if we believe in both what Christ *said* and what he *demonstrated*, we can believe that what we call 'death' is only the gateway to something infinitely more splendid and glorious than we can at present imagine.

If the weight of our faith rests upon Christ and his promises, we do not allow this present life either to deceive or defeat us. Our faith lies in what we cannot at present see.

It adds a new dimension to our living, if we believe that this life is a preparation for something much more important.

It is of immense comfort to know that those who are taken from our sight are even more alive in a higher stage of existence.

❖

27 March

DEATH CONQUERED!

A lot of people nowadays refuse to believe that there is any such place as heaven—or hell for that matter. To believe that we go on living after death is just wishful thinking—it is simply that we cannot bear the thought of ceasing to exist, so we invent a dream world of continued existence which we call heaven.

So death *is* the end!

It does seem an awful waste! Everything that a man was, every scrap of personality or character which he possessed or achieved, all his hopes and ideals just finish when the poor old body dies.

Apparently the wooden box and the six feet of earth are the end of life for everybody.

But death has, of course, been conquered!

That is what Christians believe.

Enthusiastically.

❖

28 March

'WHEN YOU'RE DEAD...'

'When you're dead, you're dead' is a kind of motto of the materialistic welfare state. It gives you permission to pursue every kind of personal pleasure since this life is all you have got. It relieves you of a good deal of moral responsibility since nobody lives beyond the grave. Heaven, hell and judgment are merely bogeys which frightened past generations.

Yet there lurks in the heart of a great many people the hope, if not the belief, that death is not the end. I have seen many people die and I have seen many others in the presence of the death of someone whom they love. My experience is that it is very rare indeed to find that the attitude summed up in the words 'when you're dead, you're dead', is still there *in the actual presence of death*.

Jesus rose again to prove that death was not the end. Because of his startling demonstration of life after public execution, a great new faith was born into the world.

It has continued until today.

❖

29 March

'YOU CAN'T DIE!'

You cannot be surprised that these early Christians were not in the least afraid of death.

Jesus promised them, as he still promises us, that those whose life is entrusted to him will pass through death as surely as he did. The early Christians only had to believe their eyes—the matter was demonstrated in front of their faces.

Millions of Christians today also believe that the great event really happened. The strange thing is that, when you do put your faith in Jesus Christ—not the faraway figure in history, but the Christ who is alive today—you too feel that death is only an incident.

All the hopes and inklings of your heart confirm this.

The 'wishful thinking' becomes an unshakeable conviction.

You can't die, for you are linked to the permanent life of God through Jesus Christ.

The body can die, like anything else in this perishing world.

You can't.

✤

30 March

GOD'S DIVE

Any religion worthy of the name makes an attempt, however pathetic or misdirected, to effect a rapprochement between man and the goodness of God. So, quickly or slowly, it dawns on the Christian that he is himself quite powerless to do anything in the matter. Yet overlaid by the cushioning and veneers of civilization there still exists in modern man a latent sense that 'something ought to be done about it'. One day (and it may then be a soul-shattering experience) it breaks upon the Christian that the 'something which ought to be done' has been done by Christ on the cross. He sees that God is not so much a God 'of purer eyes than to behold iniquity' (which sounds to me like a maiden aunt who would avert her head from anything rude or unpleasant) but a God who did the only possible thing. So far from staying aloof, he took what C.S. Lewis calls 'that tremendous dive' and became a human being. And not only that, but this incredible God of ours allowed the forces of evil to close in upon him and kill him—an unimaginable agony this.

To put it crudely, God endured an almost incredible conflict within his own Godhead, to reconcile men to himself.

What was done once in time and space is a focusing on the screen of human history what is eternally happening in the heart of God.

Even to contemplate this for a moment takes the Christian's breath away.

31 March

HE HAS BEEN HERE

The Christian faith is founded upon no mere system of ideals or exhortations to lead a good life, and certainly not upon a beautiful myth. Its foundation is a well-attested, sober fact of history; that quietly but with deliberate purpose God himself has visited this little planet.

Some people get very excited on the subject of flying saucers and who indeed could fail to be thrilled if it were known for certain that creatures from another planet had succeeded in visiting our own? But *our* faith begins with something infinitely more thrilling—that God himself has visited our earth in Person.

Indeed he measured his stature to fit our needs, and made his entry in humility and obscurity.

We can say with the utmost confidence, 'He has been here.'

Thank God, the God and Father of our Lord Jesus Christ, that in his great mercy we men have been born again into a life full of hope, through Christ's rising again from the dead! You can now hope for a perfect inheritance beyond the reach of change and decay, reserved in heaven for you. And in the meantime you are guarded by the power of God operating through your faith, till you enter fully into the salvation which is all ready to be revealed at the last. This means tremendous joy to you, even though at present you may be temporarily harassed by all kinds of trials.

1 PETER 1:3–6

April

The proof of God's amazing love is this: that it was while we were sinners that Christ died for us. Moreover, if he did that for us while we were sinners, now that we are men justified by the shedding of his blood, what reason have we to fear the wrath of God? If, while we were his enemies, Christ reconciled us to God by dying for us, surely now that we are reconciled we may be perfectly certain of our salvation through his living in us. Nor, I am sure, is this a matter of bare salvation—we may hold our heads high in the light of God's love because of the reconciliation which Christ has made.

ROMANS 5:8–11

✣

1 April

THE REVERBERATING MIRACLE

The birth of Jesus Christ is a well-attested fact of history, but, of course, it became that, for the most part, in retrospect. For as the holy babe grew to manhood it was only here and there that men recognized what they were seeing—God focused in human form.

When the final tragedy came and the forces of darkness conspired to put out the Light, probably a mere handful retained their faith. It was the reverberating miracle of the resurrection, witnessed and vouched for by hundreds of reliable witnesses, which settled the matter, and transformed dispirited disciples into determined heroes prepared to challenge and change the world. Convinced now (who wouldn't be after such a demonstration with the last enemy of man?), the young Church could look back and say with every confidence, 'Now we know that this was indeed the Son of God!'

No doubt there were many times when these early Christians meditated on the strangely quiet entry of God into his world, but as we read of their vigour and joy in the book of The Acts, we find them proclaiming not Christmas, but 'Jesus and the resurrection'. Not only were his own claims justified to the hilt. Not only was the dark bogey of death resoundingly defeated. This Man was alive and with them!

They knew his power in their lives.

They knew for certain that in the living God-become-Man lay the power to rescue, forgive and transform anybody.

2 April

ATONEMENT UNLIMITED

The moment we begin to use technical terms to describe the atonement or strive to reduce this extraordinary activity of God into a theological formula, the life goes out of it. At best it becomes a hoary and venerated super fairy story. At worst it is the plaything and battleground of amateur theologians.

If we believe this atonement to be a historical fact and an everlasting fact, then we cannot limit its effect backwards or forwards in time or even, so to speak, sideways.

I have no doubt that all that human goodness and unselfish effort which goes under the name of 'humanism' is as much a fruit of the cross of Christ as a church prayer meeting.

We dare not limit the effects of reconciliation to those who can advance and subscribe to a certain theory of atonement.

If we regard the atonement as a tremendous action from the Godward side to rescue man from his predicament, we must beware of limiting its effects.

✢

3 April

THE HUMILITY OF GOD

The life of Jesus often fulfilled many Old Testament prophecies about him, but once at least, he quite deliberately arranged such a fulfilment. He rode into Jerusalem on a donkey in order to fulfil the prophecy of Zechariah: 'Behold, thy King cometh meek and sitting upon an ass.'

Jesus' choice of the poor man's beast to carry him into the Holy City was an acted parable of the humility of the coming of the King of kings.

Jesus was largely unrecognized for what he was because of his lack of pomp and splendour. I suspect that even John the Baptist, that fearless messenger who prepared the way of the Lord, had doubts about Jesus as he lay in prison. He had heralded a mighty King who should come with power and judgment, so there came that poignant message from the dungeon: 'Art thou he that should come or do we look for another?'

The message Jesus sent back to him was the calm reassurance that the King had come in power and judgment but with neither the form of power nor of judgment that John had expected.

The humility of God is a hard thing to accept and believe.

✢

4 April

THE POWER OF HUMILITY

John, recording an incident which he found unforgettable, and which is unforgettable, writes that 'Jesus, knowing that he came from God and went to God, took a towel and girded himself and began to wash the disciples' feet' (John 13:3–4).

We are so accustomed to thinking of power in relation to force that we find it hard to believe that the greatest power of all could show the greatest conceivable humility. Yet in fact, 'the Word became flesh and dwelt among us' (John 1:14). The King of kings and Lord of lords stepped willingly out of the shining magnificence of the eternal world to be born and laid in a manger. It is the same breathtaking humility again.

This is not an acted humility but a real humility. This we must remember. It is equally important that we should realize in a world that worships power and success and outward splendour that such humility cannot be despised or disregarded. The Baby laid in a manger did not live a particularly distinguished life by worldly standards and his death was the death of a common criminal. Yet there is no character which has attracted such worldwide loyalty and no authority which has commanded such willing devotion.

✢

5 April

FORGIVENESS FREE

A great many people resent the declared fact that they can do absolutely nothing to reconcile themselves to God, however hard they try. Human pride is intensely hostile to the fact that God himself has effected the reconciliation of the world to himself through Christ. People hate to think that no amount of good works or even self-sacrifice can win or deserve God's favour. Forgiveness, acceptance, restoration (whatever we call it) is a *gift*.

To some that is hard to take.

Sometimes, through the sheer painful experiences of life, men and women come to realize that they *need* the love and forgiveness of God and that there is nothing they can do to earn it. Sometimes at the end of years of painful fruitless searching after truth, they have to drop all their pretences and accept the simple Gospel message of God's forgiveness.

There are famous people who have put it on record that the one thing they could not accept about Christianity was its starting-point, the acceptance of God's forgiveness.

In the end, however, each man or woman has to reach the same conclusion.

We are all sinners who need the grace and restoration of God's free forgiveness.

✤

6 April

THE HILL OF GOLGOTHA

See in your mind's eye, the hill of Golgotha.

The cries of mockery, the jeers and taunts have long since died away. The fearful heat, which had beaten upon the prisoners, pitilessly exposed in their agony, has given place at noon to a sudden chill. For three long hours a strange darkness has covered the countryside. The birds, in this false night, have fallen silent. Many of the onlookers have drawn their cloaks around them in the growing cold and drifted quietly back to Jerusalem.

It is an eerie scene. The countryside, usually hard and bright in the sunshine, lies in mysterious shadow. Apart from the Roman guard, very few of either friends or foes of the figure on the central cross remain there.

The centurion thinks a few of the man's followers are stealing back to watch from a safe distance. His own men are restive. They are rough soldiers and, like most rough and tough men, intensely superstitious. They mutter to whatever gods or goddesses they believe in, as they shift uneasily from one foot to another.

The centurion feels a growing conviction that this man on the middle cross is being unjustly, as well as cruelly, executed.

Feels it intensely.

✣

7 April

THE END OF THE WORLD

No one is put in charge of a hundred men in the Roman Imperial Army unless he is a shrewd judge of men, thinks the centurion. The other two poor wretches on their crosses are ordinary highway robbers, who would have slit your throat as readily as they would slit your purse. They are getting their deserts. But this man—a truly good man if ever he had seen one—does not deserve a death like this.

Perhaps this darkness is a sign of the wrath of whatever gods there are.

The centurion remembers old campaigners in the regiment, who had travelled widely over the vast empire, telling him of similar times of the sun's growing dark in the daytime. Always, he remembered they had told him, the natives had gone crazy thinking that they had mortally offended the gods and that the end of the world had come!

But this is none of his business, he reminds himself.

His job is to see that the prisoners die, and that no man rescues them.

✣

8 April

FRUITLESS MOCKERY

From time to time the centurion has to speak sharply to his men, reminding them to keep alert.

It is possible that the followers of this young preacher might seize the opportunity of darkness to make a desperate attempt to rescue this man Jesus, although by now he must certainly be almost dead. Then, as he remembers those followers, his soldierly lip curls in contempt. When this man had needed them most, they had all fled. Cowards they were, indeed.

After three hours of this uncanny darkness, the silence is almost complete. At first the jeers and abuse from the bystanders had risen even above the dreadful screams and curses of the agonized thieves. But as time passed and the strength of the victims ebbed, their cries had died down to groans and whimpering. Now, apart from an occasional sighing moan, they hang there silent.

The abuse of the bloodthirsty crowd at the man Jesus has died away completely.

For one thing he had not answered them back by as much as one word.

After a time, even the most brutal will grow tired of fruitless mockery.

✛

9 April

THE MAN IN THE MIDDLE

When the darkness came, and they made for home, some were beating their breasts, as Jews do in times of sorrow. Perhaps there had been something in the dignity and bearing of the central figure, which even transcended the humiliation of his stripped and beaten body, and this had touched a heart here and there.

When a human heart has raged and railed against a helpless victim, when the fury and the spleen are all spent, there will sometimes come a strange reaction. Perhaps, thought some of those who returned with bowed heads to their homes, it is we who have been shamed. Perhaps it is we who are in the wrong.

The centurion glances up at the three figures. The two thieves, he reflects grimly, are nearly out of it. All their cursing and blaspheming and writhing have exhausted them. But what of this man in the middle? He has wasted no strength, and, despite the dreadful flogging of a few hours ago, he has a strong body.

He may linger until the last beastly business of breaking the legs has to be done. The centurion hopes fervently this will not be so. Brave men do not deserve to die like this.

Again the feeling comes into his heart that this man was both immensely brave and completely innocent.

Perhaps he was even more than an ordinary man.

Perhaps he was a son of one of the gods.

÷

10 April

HE THINKS OF OTHERS

This man haunts the centurion strangely. He asked his God to forgive those who were doing this unspeakable thing to him. While he himself had not heard the actual words, he had seen him speak, probably a few words of comfort, to one of the thieves, even though both of them had been hurling curses at him a few minutes before. It was plain that the thief had received some kind of comfort, even in his excruciating pain.

Then there had been those words spoken to the woman still standing at the foot of the cross, who, he had been told, was the man's mother. There was something about that young man, who is with her now, looking after her and giving her a home.

Pain of this kind brings out the worse in men. They curse and scream at friend and foe alike, just as even a favourite dog will turn on his master with bared fangs if the pain is great enough. But not this man. Even in this hell of torture, he thinks of others.

A soldier has his duty to do.

He is not paid to take sides, except in battle.

He must never allow himself the luxury of pity.

He must therefore pull himself together.

11 April

'MY GOD, MY GOD…'

The great darkness is beginning to lift. He looks up at the face of the man whose head was still crowned with those wicked spikes of thorn, and looks away.

This was a young man, but the face he had just seen looked as though it had borne every sorrow and pain since the world began. The eyes are open and looking heavenwards. The dry cracked lips move pitiably, then, suddenly, a great resounding shout comes from that man who had been silent for so long.

'*Eloi, Eloi, lama sabachthani*,' he cries (Mark 15:34).

The Hebrew words echo back from the rocks.

This, apparently the first admission of defeat, the first sign of the cracking of a human spirit, aroused the few cruel mockers who were still on the scene. They obviously knew as little of the Hebrew tongue as the centurion himself.

'Listen,' they cry, 'he's calling for Elijah! The poor chap's mind is going.'

Some of them, at last moved by pity, run to fetch a sponge and some sour wine and a stick so that they can reach the parched lips. But the coarser spirits among them said, 'No, let him alone. Let's wait and see if Elijah really does come and rescue him.'

But there was no rescue.

Those who love Jesus, those who watch at a safe distance know the meaning of this cry.

It is part of a psalm they had known since childhood.

'My God, my God, why hast thou forsaken me?' was the cry.

✜

12 April

A CRY OF RELIEF

The significance of the question 'My God, my God, why hast thou forsaken me?' shouted 'in a great voice', at the end of three hours of darkness, is important. It is not to be interpreted as the cry of a soul lost in the anguish of desolation.

The Hebrew words were translated by Mark (or possibly first by Peter) into Greek, and in that language, the use of the aorist tense carries the force of, 'Why *didst* thou forsake me?'

That translation is in accordance with the sense of the actual words which Jesus spoke. So this strange cry may well have been one of unspeakable relief.

The darkness and the desolation had been borne in silence but were now passing away. The dreadful spiritual agony, to which we must return in a moment, had been endured. That cup of suffering which the Son of God had feared and dreaded, and from which he had prayed so desperately to be delivered if it were possible, had now been drained to its last bitter drop.

But the experience had been fearful, and the words which came to the mind of Jesus were words directly quoted from a familiar psalm.

I believe there is no note of reproach or despair in these words, but only a shuddering relief as the darkness began to lift.

'My God, my God, why didst thou forsake me?'

✤

13 April

'FOR ME'

What awful truth lies behind the inspired words of Paul when he wrote, 'He hath made him to be sin for us, who knew no sin: that we might be made the righteousness of God in him'? It is a brutal statement, and on the face of it, so desperately unjust. Yet countless millions, down the centuries and throughout the world, have found their relationship with God restored in accepting a sacrifice which they would always be powerless to make.

Every time we come to Holy Communion, we receive broken bread to represent his sorely wounded body, and poured-out wine to represent the blood that he shed. And this we are commanded to do until he comes again, lest we forget the cost at which the bridge between God and man was built and the reconciliation finally made.

To some this seems a monstrous, even an immoral, doctrine. How, they ask, can we blithely accept the atoning action of someone else for sins for which we ourselves are responsible? But if God has not made the reconciliation, who can?

Every religion in the world worth serious consideration makes some attempt to remove this dreadful impasse. How can there be reconciliation between the utter perfection of God and the sins and guilt of mankind?

Countless thousands since Paul's day have found their peace in the 'atoning work' of Christ. They can only be grateful, as he was, to 'the Son of God, who loved me and gave himself *for me*'.

We are in the presence of a very great mystery.

✤

14 April

'WE CANNOT TELL...'

Another reason for this unique mental and spiritual agony goes deeper still.

Some time before the crucifixion, John the Baptist, with that insight which is the stamp of every true prophet, had exclaimed, 'Behold the Lamb of God, which taketh away the sin of the world' (John 1:29). I cannot pretend even now, after many years in the ministry of the Church, that I understand the meaning of atonement. I only know that the Representative Man deliberately allowed the forces of evil to close in upon him, and, in the end, to kill him.

Long ago the Irish hymn writer, Mrs Alexander, wrote:

> *We may not know, we cannot tell*
> *What pains he had to bear...*

I confess I do not know, nor can I tell.

I only know that what you and I could never do was done for us, at infinite cost, upon the cross.

✤

15 April

ASKING QUESTIONS

It was characteristic of Jesus to *ask a question*, even at such a time. All great personalities have their own traits, and the greatest of all human personalities was no exception. Have you noticed how often Jesus used a question, where we might have expected a statement?

The more we love and understand something of his mind, the more we see the profound wisdom of his method.

When Jesus was asked a question, again and again we find him asking a counter-question—often a haunting as well as a penetrating one—which does its own work as men try to answer it.

Think on the following examples.

'*Why* are ye so fearful?' he asked the terrified disciples in the storm-tossed fishing boat (Mark 4:40). Indeed why are you and I so often fearful? To answer that question properly takes us to the very root of our being, to the fundamental relationship between ourselves and God.

On another occasion Jesus said to his enemies, 'Why go ye about to kill me?' (John 7:19). We simply do not know whether his enemies were forced by that piercing question to examine their own hearts. We only know that the more vocal of them hotly protested that they had no murderous intent, even though in fact, they did succeed in getting him put to death. But (and this is a recorded fact which I have found many Christians have overlooked) we read in Acts 6:7 that 'a great company of the priests (in Jerusalem) were obedient to the faith'.

It is highly probable that among these were men whose spirits had been stabbed awake by a simple question.

✢

16 April

'WHY, OH WHY...?'

The most remarkable question of all was spoken by Christ himself, not now on earth but risen and ascended. It was spoken to Saul, the man who had wrought such cruel havoc on the men and women of the early Church. What untold damage this one fanatical Pharisee had done! And yet he is brought up short on the road to Damascus, not by any word of condemnation or blame, but in a blinding moment of truth, by a simple question: 'Saul, Saul, *why* are you persecuting me?' (Acts 9:4).

When it struck the heart of one as fiercely honest with himself as Saul of Tarsus, the result was explosive.

I sometimes feel that, when we are quiet before the living Christ, he meets us, sinners as we are, not with blame and reproach but with a penetrating question of some kind. We must never be so busy with our prayers and devotions that we drown the voice of Jesus. Nor must we be so busy in our lives that we have no time to reply to what he is asking, or to let that reply influence our daily business of living.

✢

17 April

THE RIGHT QUESTIONS

This same Jesus has a habit of asking the right questions.

We find him as a boy of twelve asking questions in the Temple.

We find him in his brief but crowded ministry asking questions.

We find him after the anguish, the loneliness and the despair, asking that care-ful question, 'My God, my God, why didst thou forsake me?' In the light of what we know of his habit of asking questions, it is not irreverent to suggest that there was a purpose in the asking of that question too. Those who first heard it must have wondered how to answer it. As we watch the divine Passion two thousand years later, we too must surely make an attempt to answer it.

Why *did* the Perfect Man experience not merely physical agony, but that far more deadly thing—the sense of having been deserted by the Father with whom he had enjoyed unbroken communion all his life? The answer must be in this direction.

I believe that the Man who is our example as well as our Saviour 'was in all points tempted like as we are' (Hebrews 4:15), but in this instance infinitely more severely. It was the last chance the principalities and powers from the headquarters of evil would ever have to attack the Son of God.

The attacks of the Evil One are intermittent—even after the

temptation in the wilderness, there was a respite. But crowded into these three hours of darkness there was such a concentrated assault of evil, such blackness of soul and sense of utter dereliction that even the Man who had lived his life in perfect faith and obedience cried out as he did *when at last it was over*.

18 April

LIGHT IN THE TUNNEL

There are diseases of the body which produce depression of mind, a phenomenon which many of us have experienced after recovering from influenza or some other virus infection. The colour, the meaning and the point of life simply disappear for a time. We pray apparently to an empty heaven, and in our misery we torture ourselves by brutal self-condemnation. There are however those who have to endure such conditions month after month, and even year after year. We who know something of God's love can truly help them by our love and our prayers. There is light at the end of their dark tunnel. In the meantime we may help them far more by our encouragement than perhaps we know.

Sometimes those of us who are not experts in the treatment of mental illness can do no more than stand by and pray. But it is heartening to remember that such black depression, such utter desolation, fell upon the sinless Son of God.

He who is now ascended up on high, taking our humanity with him, as it were, can be relied upon not to have forgotten his own agony.

We can pray, in the name of the Man who went through the same thing himself, for those who feel themselves cut off from God.

✣

19 April

THIS COSTLY ACT

What are we to make of such astonishing statements as that he (Jesus) 'should taste death for every man' (Hebrews 2:9), or that 'God was in Christ, reconciling the world unto himself' (2 Corinthians 5:19)?

Thousands of books have been written to explain the mystery, and I must have read hundreds of them. My appreciation of the costly act itself has grown with the years, but I cannot, in all honesty, say that I am much nearer understanding so perilous and costly a mystery.

The more I think of it and the more I allow my imagination to fill in the gaps in the terse Gospel narratives, the less I am surprised that 'from the sixth hour there was darkness over the land unto the ninth hour' (Mark 15:33). God only knows what fearful battles were being grimly fought, or what agonies were being silently endured in that time.

All I am certain of is this: the ordeal was endured, the battle was won, and through Christ we are free men who can approach our Father with confidence.

But sometimes my blood still runs cold when I try to imagine what experience it was that wrung from our Lord the cry—even though it may have been a cry of relief, 'My God, my God, why didst thou forsake me?'

✣

20 April

THE EMPTY TOMB

It does not worry me in the least that the man whom God had proved to be his Christ, and to whom he had given 'all power in heaven and in earth' should use his 'resurrection body' in any way that he chose.

There are such things as visions and there are hallucinations, but the more I study the evidence, the more I am convinced that Jesus was raised from the dead, body and all, in a real sense, leaving an open tomb and empty grave-clothes.

✣

21 April

NO OLD WIVES' TALE

The resurrection is, as I say, a historic fact for me. Death, which all men instinctively fear, is, as we have seen, a conquered enemy. Paul saw the power required to overcome man's 'last enemy' as the same power which transformed godless and hopeless pagans into heroes of faith and endurance.

I cannot believe anyone was changed by 'idle tales' or 'cunningly devised fables'.

The pagan world had a surfeit of myths and fables, and one more would not have been noticed. But this was fact, dramatic, exciting, potent and life-giving. You could not expect men and women in pagan cities like Corinth and Ephesus to risk their livelihood and sometimes their lives for an old wives' tale.

Even less would you expect a man like Paul, with his keen intellect and rigorous pharisaic training, to be changed by anything less than a direct action of God within the context of human history.

Only reality could do a thing like that.

22 April

DEATH ABOLISHED

'Jesus Christ hath abolished death,' wrote Paul many years ago (2 Timothy 1:10), but there have been very few since his day who appear to have believed it. The power of the dark old god, rooted no doubt in instinctive fear, is hard to shake, and a great many Christian writers, though possessing the brightest hopes of 'life hereafter', cannot, it seems, accept the abolition of death.

'The valley of the shadow', 'death's gloomy portal', 'the bitter pains of death', and a thousand other expressions all bear witness to the fact that a vast number of Christians do not really believe what Christ said.

Probably the greatest offender is John Bunyan, writing in his *Pilgrim's Progress* of the 'icy river' through which the pilgrims must pass before they reach the Celestial City. Thousands, possibly millions, must have been influenced in their impressionable years by reading *Pilgrim's Progress*. Yet the 'icy river' is entirely a product of Bunyan's own fears, and the New Testament will be searched in vain for the slightest endorsement of his idea.

To 'sleep in Christ', to 'depart and be with Christ', 'to fall asleep'—these are the expressions the New Testament uses.

It is high time the 'icy river', 'the gloomy portal', 'the bitter pains', and all the rest of the melancholy images were brought face to face with the fact:

'Jesus Christ hath abolished death.'

23 April

ALIVE—AND SEEN

Some years before the writing of any of the four Gospels, a letter was despatched by Paul to a small group of Christians in Corinth. Among other remarkable things in that letter, Paul states that the man Jesus had shown himself alive, after his crucifixion, to individual people. In addition he was observed to be alive after death by a group of five hundred people simultaneously.

Of these, Paul comments, the majority are still alive, although some have passed away in the intervening twenty-five years.

This statement in 1 Corinthians 15:6 is part of the absolute conviction of Paul that he was worshipping no dead hero but a living person. In the rough pagan world of those days, a man who declared himself a believer in Jesus Christ might suffer all kinds of loss, persecution or even death. But the unique event which proved to him the claims of Jesus, and took away from him the fear of death was well attested.

No one ever produced any proof that Jesus had not really died, not that the resurrection was a put-up job. In fact the strength and vitality of the young Church lay in its certainty that Jesus had overcome death and opened to all who believed in him, a share in the timeless life of God.

24 April

A GHOST EATING!

There is an almost haphazard recording of the appearances of Jesus after his resurrection, which I find extraordinarily convincing. I think my favourite again occurs in Luke's work.

When the two who were walking to Emmaus had rushed back to Jerusalem to report their astounding experience to the eleven, they found that they already knew that 'the Lord is risen indeed and hath appeared to Simon' (Luke 24:34).

Again, according to Luke, while they are still talking excitedly Jesus himself appears among them. They were, as we might say, scared out of their wits. They thought they were seeing a ghost. But Jesus reassures them and, as was his habit, he asks penetrating questions. 'Why are you so worried?' 'Why do doubts arise in your minds? Look at my hands and my feet—it is really I myself! Feel and see: ghosts have no flesh or bones as you can see that I have.'

Then Luke makes his shrewd comment as a doctor and student of human nature. 'They still could not believe it through sheer joy and were quite bewildered' (Luke 24:41). There follows this extraordinary, and, in a way, amusing test of whether Jesus really was there in person.

He asks them, 'Have you anything here to eat?' We can imagine the frantic dash to a shelf or cupboard where they kept their food, and we can imagine that they saw no incongruity in offering him a piece of broiled fish and part of a honeycomb. But I myself cannot imagine that Jesus consumed this rather strange meal before their eyes without a smile! But this in a way clinched it; whoever heard of a ghost eating?

I find this is the kind of story which no man would invent, but which a man who was present would remember until his dying day.

And Luke, bless him, records it.

✣

25 April

NOT IN A CORNER!

It was against a background of broken hope and utter despair that the great miracle of resurrection occurred.

All four evangelists spend quite a lot of their short narratives in recounting the betrayal, the mock-trial, the final humiliations and the criminal execution.

I do not think this was done merely for dramatic effect.

It was written to show what even the best of men could suffer in this evil world.

It was written to show all who should follow Jesus that he was not God pretending to be a man, but God who had become a man.

The resounding triumph of the resurrection was therefore all the more splendid and magnificent. Armed with no supernatural equipment, Jesus had conquered man's last enemy, death. He had shown beyond all possible doubt that the victory was complete.

To live again was no longer a pious hope or a wishful thought; it was a certainty.

No conspiracy, no trick, no hysterical vision was responsible for this new certainty.

As Paul remarked crisply some years later to King Agrippa, 'this thing was not done in a corner' (Acts 26:26).

✛

26 April

ALWAYS THERE

It was of the greatest importance that the disciples should realize that Jesus had, in every sense, defeated and conquered death.

It is true that, over a period of some weeks, he had to show them that, whether they could see him or not, he was always with them. But they must not think of him as an apparition or a disembodied spirit. Therefore the empty tomb; therefore the times when these men were allowed to touch and handle the body which had passed through death; therefore, as they remembered afterwards, he sometimes ate ordinary food with them after his resurrection.

But little by little the bodily contacts grew less. The ascension was a simple and telling way of showing that no more physical demonstration could be expected.

With the promise of his continued presence and the equally certain promise of his own Spirit which was to come upon them, we are not surprised to read that the disciples returned to Jerusalem 'with great joy'.

✣

27 April

NO NONSENSE!

Why does Paul insist on a 'body' at all? It is because he is concerned to defend the Christian belief in man's resurrection after the pattern of Christ's resurrection.

The resurrection of Christ was always, for Paul, the key to the human dilemma. Christ had become a man, Christ had died for man, and Christ had risen to open the door to the glories that the human vocabulary has no words to describe. Paul knew that man's last enemy, death, was now defeated, and men could look forward, not to a shadowy half-life, but to one fuller and more glorious than human imagination can conceive.

No more nonsense, he urges in his letter to the Corinthians, about what sort of 'body' we shall possess when these mortal bodies perish. That we can safely leave to God, who has demonstrated the defeat of death by the raising up of Christ.

✣

28 April

A SPIRITUAL BODY

Some people in Paul's time, as some people now, seemed to envisage this temporary corruptible body being magically revived, and to think that this is what is meant by 'resurrection'. It isn't. Paul is at pains to explain that, even on this planet, the 'body' which contains the life is adapted to the environment—fish, birds, animals are all different, while the 'celestial bodies' to be observed in the sky are completely and splendidly unlike anything earthly.

God gives us the 'spiritual' body suitable for the new environment for which we are destined as sons of God. We can be sure of that. The resurrection of Christ is our guarantee.

We can be equally sure that 'the transitory could never possess the everlasting' (1 Corinthians 15:50). Indeed who would wish for this old, weary, diseased, and possibly maimed body to be somehow newly injected with life?

❖

29 April

INASMUCH...

Christ was drastically practical. I am pretty sure of what he says to us when we make our strictures and censures on the conduct of the world around us. He is saying (and I speak reverently), 'Well, what are *you* doing about it?'

The burdens and complexities of the world's sorrows are so great that no man can bear them all, or even imagine them all. But that is no excuse for doing nothing.

If we lay ourselves open to the love of God, there is no doubt at all that he will give us a 'concern' for a particular part of his whole vast scheme of redeeming mankind. It may be a public and exciting thing that God calls you to, or it may be humdrum and obscure. But if we are truly Christian, we cannot avoid this aspect of the cross. We have got to give *ourselves*, our time, our talents, above all, our hearts, in expressing our love for God in concern and love for our fellow men.

It *is* true, and it will *always* be true that 'inasmuch as we do it to the least of his brethren we do it to him'.

30 April

LIFE ETERNAL

The woman at the well (John 4) was told that the man who believed in Jesus Christ would have in himself 'a spring of water welling up into everlasting life'.

The Christian faith teaches that everlasting life is a sharing in the life of God. So long as a man is self-centred, earthbound, he has no particular reason, so far as I can see, to believe in survival and still less of sharing God's eternal life. But if through Christ, 'God become-man', he is linked in heart and mind to the eternal God, he already shares something of God's permanent life and cannot die.

'I am the Resurrection and the Life... He that liveth and believeth in me shall never die' (John 11:25).

'Jesus Christ hath abolished death' (2 Timothy 1:10).

'If a man keep my sayings, he shall never see death' (John 8:51–52).

Do not take all this with a pinch of salt.

It is literally true.

Death is a negligible experience to the one whose faith and trust are in Christ.

✣

Easter

THE GLORY OF EASTER

We may search our New Testaments in vain for any of the gloomy graveyard images, the shadows, the darkness, the pains, the bitterness of death, which still appear in many of our Christian hymns. There is no death for the Christian; it has, as I have emphasized repeatedly, been completely abolished. For the old dark god with his weapons of basic, primitive fear still operates, quite illegitimately, in many Christian hearts.

We should allow him no foothold, for he has no right to be there, and he has no real power over us.

The glory of Easter is not a pious hope that we shall somehow survive after a fear-ridden journey through the 'gloomy portal'. It is a demonstration of undiluted joy. Christ is the one who bore the sin, the darkness, the terror, and the pain. He is the one who 'tasted death for every man'.

Must we always dim and tarnish the glory of God's magnificent promises with our mental reservations and our secret fears?

What stops us from accepting the simple fact that 'Jesus Christ hath abolished death'?

Rejoice in the glory of Easter!

✣

We can be sure that the risen Christ never dies again—death's power to master him is finished. He died, because of sin, once: he lives for God for ever. In the same way look upon yourself as dead to the appeal and power of sin but alive to God through Christ Jesus our Lord.

ROMANS 6:9–11

May

You cannot, indeed, be a Christian at all unless you have something of his Spirit in you. Now if Christ does live within you his presence means that your sinful nature is dead, but your spirit becomes alive because of the righteousness he brings with him. Once the Spirit of him who raised Christ Jesus from the dead lives within you he will, by that Spirit, bring to your whole being, yes even your mortal bodies, new strength and vitality... All who follow the leading of God's Spirit are God's own sons... The Spirit himself endorses our inward conviction that we really are the children of God.

ROMANS 8:9–16

✛

1 May

HE ASCENDED

It has always seemed to me that the Ascension of our Lord is something of a poor relation among the festivals of the Church's year, yet Paul was not uttering a truism when he said, 'Now that he ascended, what is it but that he also descended first...?' (Ephesians 4:9). If we really believe that human life was invaded from heaven by God's becoming a human being, it is surely not unreasonable to believe that the complement to that celestial 'dive' of rescue is an ascension back in triumph to heaven.

The Man who was also God had accomplished his mission. He had founded the Kingdom. He had effected the reconciliation between God and man. He had defeated man's last enemy, death. The ascension not only satisfies the mind by completing the divine work, but it strengthens and encourages the Christian soul.

Human beings look up to God, and to what Paul calls 'the heavenly', whether they are aware that they live on a spherical globe or not. Thus it was natural for Jesus, his work accomplished, to leave his followers by this acted parable.

The Man whom the early Christians had seen die and rise again did not simply vanish from their sight, as he had done on several occasions since his resurrection. He visibly ascended.

The simplest witness could understand the obvious meaning of this action, while the wisest could ponder long over its deeper significance.

⁘

2 May

ASCENSION JOY

Let us look at this acted parable a little more closely.

I know it takes a little time for human minds to assimilate a stupendous new truth. Thus, as I say, we find Jesus appearing and disappearing over a period of some six weeks. During this time he is not only teaching his disciples, but helping them to grow accustomed to the idea that he is with them, and indeed will be in them, whether he is visible or not.

Eventually the time comes when Jesus must show the disciples as directly, simply and kindly as possible that, as a bodily presence such as they knew in the streets and on the hills of Palestine, he is to be no more with them. What could more plainly and finally convey to the men of those days this departure than the simple event of the ascension?

There is no question of a 'countdown' and a 'blast-off'! In the act of blessing them the man, whom they knew and loved, rose there on the hill side until 'a cloud received him out of their sight'.

This is what they saw. This is what they later reported to Luke, but it is not to be explained or explained away in terms of modern physics. Nevertheless it must have been an extraordinarily satisfying experience for these early disciples since they, according to Luke, 'returned to Jerusalem with great joy'.

They knew now for certain that death had been conquered.

They knew that their beloved Jesus was truly the Son of God.

Ringing in their ears was the promise that they would be given the power to go out and to tell the world that 'Christ is risen', that 'Christ is alive in power'.

This surely was Ascension joy!

✣

3 May

TARRY!

The early apostles were told to 'tarry until' they were 'endued with power from on High'. Pentecost, when it came, was unique in the history of the Church, but it is still true that we need to 'tarry', to wait quietly in faith and expectation if we are to wield something of the power of God in actual down-to-earth human situations.

Our tendency is to rush in with our wisdom, our experience, our common sense, our sympathy, and so on. None of these is valueless, but, again and again, I have observed how strangely ineffective they are to deal with a difficult situation outside ourselves, unless they are guided and empowered by the Spirit of God.

I do not suggest that we are simply to wait for a feeling of power from on high, or that we are to despise the ordinary gifts of personality which God has given us. What I am suggesting is that these gifts are infinitely more effectual if in simple faith we believe that there is such a thing as the power of God (whether we feel it or not) and that we spend time regularly opening our spirits to that source of all spiritual power.

4 May

PENTECOST

Pentecost *was* unique. Even in the ensuing pages of the New Testament we read of nothing like that happening again. But we do read of the operation of that great gift of God in ways that come very close to us today. We read of 'fruits of the Spirit' which seem to be the very things most needed in our modern life.

Our modern ways of thinking do not readily accept the idea of anything coming 'from outside' into our known scheme of things. We do not mind making adjustments and alterations *within* our scheme of things, but we do not like the idea of there being anything *outside* of that scheme that we actually need. We have made such enormous strides in all branches of knowledge, and particularly in psychology, that we resent the thought that there should be any invasion of our world by any outside spiritual force.

So a message like that of Pentecost sounds very strange to the modern ear.

I am full of admiration for modern progress, but I see that the message of Pentecost is particularly relevant today.

For the Spirit of God can change human nature.

And does.

✢

5 May

THE SPIRIT OF TRUTH

We cannot turn the clock back, so it would be stupid to pretend that life anywhere in today's world is the same as the life of New Testament times. But people are the same, and the basic problems of human relationships are the same.

The Spirit which Jesus promises would lead his followers 'into all truth' is very actively at work wherever he is allowed to be so. Some of his work is painful in the extreme. There has often to be the breaking-up of old ways of thinking, the expansion of responsibility and the checking of priorities.

Anyone who opens his personality to the living Spirit takes a risk of being considerably shaken.

It seems obvious to me that the churches themselves are now being shaken too, perhaps as they have not been for centuries.

But we need not fear.

The Spirit of truth does not contradict himself.

He will lead us all into the Truth.

6 May

THE POWER OF THE SPIRIT

We should learn more for ourselves of the power of the Spirit of God. Are we a little shy of receiving this gift of God? Do we connect it in our minds only with hysteria and religious excitement?

We are quite wrong if we do that.

When Paul wrote the letter to the Galatians, he said that, in his experience, the receiving of the Spirit of God in human life showed itself in love and joy and peace. He said that there was shown a patience, a gentleness and a goodness of character that was not there before. He said that there was, too, a new faith, a new willingness to accept life, and a new self-discipline of the personality.

These are not hysterical virtues.

They are things that most of us desperately need.

For, by nature, we do not have much of these things.

7 May

ASK FOR THIS GIFT!

The Spirit of God is a gift. We cannot earn it any more than we can earn our acceptance with God. But just as we can accept the forgiveness of God, so too we can accept this spiritual and inner gift of God to make us whole and strong.

I have read many books on the Holy Spirit. Some made the receiving of this gift so complicated that no one who was not a born mystic and a religious genius—as well as having plenty of time to spare—could ever hope to receive such a gift! How unlike Jesus that is! He says things like this: 'Some of you are fathers. If your sons ask you for food, would you think of giving them a stone? Then how much more likely is your Heavenly Father to give the Holy Spirit to anyone who asks for it.'

To *anyone* who asks!

There lies the secret.

We must come to the end of our cleverness and self-sufficiency, and we must see our need of spiritual reinforcement, yes of spiritual change, before we are willing to ask.

But as we ask, we shall find that he gives.

Ask for this gift!

8 May

THE BIRTHDAY OF THE CHURCH

Christmas, according to Christianity, is the anniversary of that almost incredible act of God—his entering the stream of human life by becoming a baby. Good Friday is the anniversary of the death of the

Man that baby became. It is called 'Good' because, through that apparent tragedy, God reconciled man to himself.

Easter commemorates the historic fact that Jesus Christ conquered death and 'came back' to show in a series of unmistakable demonstrations that he had really done so.

Whitsun follows on, and is the commemoration of a special occasion on which God did, with special emphasis, something that he is always prepared to do—that is, to give some of his own personality to those who are willing to receive him.

It is therefore the birthday of the new community of men and women who joined together to achieve God's purpose by the power of his Spirit.

It is the beginning of the Christian Church.

9 May

GOD-GIVEN POWER

I find Luke's account of the beginning of the young Church strangely moving. This mere handful of early believers, who had deserted their Master the moment real danger threatened, and who had, apparently, taken so long to realize that he had really and demonstrably conquered death, are bidden to wait. They are convinced; they are full of joy. But they lack the power to breach the defences of an unbelieving world.

The story, all too familiar to many of us who have been Christians for years, is told with extraordinary simplicity and economy of words. There must be some God-given power given to that tiny band, charged with the alarming (and seemingly impossible) task of 'preaching the gospel to every creature'. And there was, for the living Spirit of God came upon these men in a way no one could have anticipated.

Luke is describing, perhaps thirty years later, something of what men told him had happened at that momentous Pentecost.

I simply cannot believe that Luke, or anybody else, concocted such a story.

✤

10 May

EXPAND!

The handful of men and women who constituted the early Church had explicit orders to expand. They had a command without limits to it: 'Go into all the world and preach the gospel to every creature' (Mark 16:15).

Some of them, and certainly St Paul, obeyed this command utterly. How often they must have been tempted to stay where they were and avoid the risk of dispersing their meagre forces, we are not told, but they must often have been tempted to remain a small, closed brotherhood.

We have not, on the whole, come anywhere near recovering the sense, so strong in the early Church, that Christ's Body is here to expand and spread; that it is in fact her standing order to 'Go into all the world and preach the gospel to every creature'. But there is now a much greater sense among church people that missions are not just a specialized part of the Church's activities in which you may or may not be interested, but are part of a Church that is living and acting throughout the whole world.

The Christian faith may appear to be marking time in Western Europe, or even losing ground, but we have only to look so far as the continent of Africa, for example, to see hundreds of young people eagerly grasping, not the white man's religion, but the Truth as it is in Jesus.

+

11 May

CERTAINTY

When the Christian faith was born, there were gods many and lords many—as St Paul says. But there was throughout the pagan world, as far as we can judge, an atmosphere of uncertainty. The old gods had largely failed and even the Jews, holding fast to their faith in the one true God, were, because of the enormous complications and accretions which had by now encrusted their religion, in a state of great uncertainty.

Into this world of darkness, swirling mists and uncertain light, there came a faith whose flame shone surely and steadily.

The Christian faith had certainty built into it. It was certain of God, certain of man's new relationship with him throughout the Gospel, certain of the living presence of Christ, and certain of life beyond the grave.

This certainly baffled the critics of the new faith. It also infuriated its persecutors.

+

12 May

TO KNOW IS TO DO

No one can be certain of God through Christ unless he is willing to do the will of God. In other words, we never know the inner voice of certainty until we are honestly committed in heart and mind to following Jesus Christ.

This is, I know, frustrating to the critics who would like to be able to assess the value of Christianity and its possible truth without in any way committing themselves. But to do that is an impossibility. You cannot *know* until you are willing to *do*.

You remember our Lord's words: 'If any man willeth to do, he shall know' (John 7:17). St John, too, in one of his Epistles, comments that the man who loves God *and is doing his will* 'hath the witness in himself' (1 John 5:10). It is not an intellectual certainty that we are seeking, but rather a certainty of the Spirit.

We can become convinced intellectually by argument or demonstration in many areas of life, but in matters of the spirit, we are convinced *only* by the Holy Spirit himself.

✣

13 May

INNER REINFORCEMENT

Without God's inner reinforcement through the Spirit, Christianity remains a beautiful ideal—which no one can live up to.

Man may admire the character of Christ, may see that his way of living is the right one, and may even try to follow him. But unless God can implant the moral power inside, the vision of being a Christian soon fades and becomes just another discarded idea.

Christianity is not meant to be a beautiful ideal which no one can live out in practice. It is the way of real, happy constructive living. It is living in harmony with God, and with our fellow men. But because of the selfishness and evil around us (and in us) we find ourselves too weak, too cowardly and too tied by past ways of thinking and feeling to embark on this real living.

This is where God comes in.

To anyone who means business and sincerely wants to live life in the new way God is prepared to give the inner reinforcement of his own Spirit.

14 May

SPIRIT-FILLED

The converts of the new faith in the early Church were an odd crowd—ex-thieves, ex-prostitutes, ex-idolaters, ex-rogues of all kinds, and a sprinkling of good-living and orthodox Jews. Yet St Paul writes to them in the confidence, not that they will make great efforts to maintain their faith, but that they may know more of the power of God working within them. He has a certain sober confidence in this internal working of the Spirit of God which it seems to me we have largely lost.

We believe in God the Father who loves us. *We* believe in God the Son who has redeemed us at the cost of his own life. *But how far do we believe in God the Holy Spirit who operates within us, conforming us into the likeness of Christ?*

We are a long way from living and behaving like Spirit-filled sons of God! Yet it appears to me that the particular and peculiar work of the invisible and very real Spirit of God is to make this change within our personalities.

It is the Spirit who teaches us, and who gently but firmly corrects us.

It is he who fills our hearts with unconquerable hope while helping us to 'conform a little more to the likeness of Christ'.

15 May

CHANGE DOES HAPPEN

How did Christ change people? Not by convincing them intellectually, but by winning their hearts to personal trust in him and personal devotion to his cause.

I do not know why a man who meets Christ will deny the love of self that has dogged his life and poisoned the springs of his life. But that does happen.

I do not know why a man can be changed in his whole attitude to life and see both the folly and wickedness of sin and the worthwhileness of serving Christ just because he comes into contact with the Spirit of Christ.

But these things are happening every day.

Christ's Spirit is still available and active today.

When we bid him entrance, we too can have the inner chambers of our hearts cleansed and set on fire with enthusiasm for his Kingdom.

✢

16 May

CHRIST IN YOU

As soon as we begin to attempt to live a life worthy of God's Fatherhood and reflecting something of his love, we become painfully aware of our own lack of resources. We have to contend with many years of wrong ways of thinking and feeling. We have to contend with the downward pull of the earthly side of our own natures and we have to contend with a surrounding atmosphere which all the time tends to destroy or minimize the new truth that has shone upon our souls. Sooner or later, and usually sooner, we realize our clamant need for inner reinforcement.

This we seek, if we are sensible, by prayer and by Bible reading and Holy Communion, and every other means of grace on which we can lay our hands.

I have a suspicion that many of us stultify these efforts by a basic lack of faith in God the Holy Spirit. I have a feeling that many people do not really believe that God himself, the Father to whom they are now reconciled, actually operates *within* their personalities.

It is as though they visualize themselves as lonely pilgrims to whom God undoubtedly vouchsafes his help in time of need, but do not see

114

themselves as sons and daughters of the Most High, not merely receiving occasional help from God, but continually indwelt by the living Spirit of God.

We tend to see God as the outward help, but to St Paul and his followers, the revolutionary thought is that Christ is *in* them, transforming their thinking and feeling, renewing their minds, inspiring their hearts, and effectually preventing them from being conformed to this fleeting world.

✛

17 May

THE LIVING SPIRIT

Jesus, anticipating his own departure from this world, promised that the Spirit of Truth should live in his followers, and should lead them into all truth. Therefore, although the Gospel records are the most historic documents in the world, the Church is promised, within its very life, the active Spirit of God himself.

If, in one sense, we do look back to the Gospels (for ours is a historic religion), in another sense it is unwise to attempt to move a contemporary situation into the setting of the Gospels two thousand years ago.

It is of course also unnecessary, *if* we believe that the living Spirit of Jesus Christ is active and operative wherever hearts and minds are ready to receive him.

18 May

THE WIND AND THE SUN

There are those who stress the primary importance of what we call the incarnation—that God became Man for us; or the crucifixion—that

Christ died for us men and for our salvation; or the resurrection—that Christ rose again to open for us the gate of everlasting life. All these things are true. They are all fundamental Christian certainties. But here is the point. The *fact* from which they spring is the nature of God himself, which is love.

Do you remember Aesop's fable about the wind and the sun?

A traveller was wearing a heavy cloak as he trudged along and the wind and the sun in the fable, each proud of his power, were sure that they could make him shed it. The wind tried first. He blew in gusts and he blew in blasts, and finally blew in a tempest of fury. But the man only hugged his cloak the tighter to him.

Then came the sun's turn. He shone benignly with pleasant warmth and then with noonday splendour, so the traveller first loosed his cloak and then flung it off altogether to bask in the heavenly sunshine.

In my own dealings with human souls, I have found that it is nearly always true that the wind of criticism and judgment and con-demnation makes a man, however great his need of God, hug the cloak of his excuses tighter. It is under the influence of the power of love and sympathy and understanding—and what delicate work this is—men will cast aside their cloaks and their defences, and even their protective harness to allow themselves to be touched by the kind and healing fingers of the love of God.

19 May

FOR OUR INNER RESOURCES

There are many things which I believe God is able and willing to provide for our inner resources. Among them is *peace*, 'peace not as the world giveth', which Christ promised.

I think of the *joy* which he also promised, for both peace and joy were promised as his gifts despite the 'persecutions' and 'tribulations' of the outside world.

I think of the promise of the Spirit himself who would 'guide us into all the truth'.

A lot has been written about 'guidance' and not all is helpful, but there are times in every Christian's life when, faced by an important decision, he feels he must know what is the purpose of God for him.

I believe that, if our hearts are open to the living Spirit of God, we shall be led, not of course like blindfold children, but as responsible sons of God, in the right way.

⁜

20 May

AS YOU THINK...

'When the will and imagination are at war, the imagination invariably gains the day': so said the famous M. Coué.

Many and many a strenuous effort of the will is frustrated by an inward picture of failure. We try desperately but if the inward picture is that of 'I knew all the time I couldn't do it', failure is inevitable.

Some say that this inward expectation is the largest factor in determining what you will actually accomplish. Your mental picture of yourself will tend to work out in practice, so that it becomes truer than ever that 'as man thinketh so is he'.

M. Coué's great message was that there should be constant suggestion of the right sort, helping us 'to be better and better every day'. His patients absorbed into their inmost imaginations the idea of health and recovery and some truly amazing cures were recorded.

The religion of Jesus Christ has in it elements of true suggestion that are of tremendous value to us in our efforts to be the 'best for God'. I am convinced that many of our efforts and really strenuous efforts are frustrated because there is an inward imagination of failure, an inner conviction that what we set out to do is really beyond us and that we are sure to fail.

If we can cherish an inward picture of ourselves actually

117

accomplishing that which we are setting out to do, we shall be immeasurably strengthened.

✤

21 May

UNCONSCIOUS CHRISTIANS

Unless a man is prepared to use his faculty of faith and grasp the fact that God is love, he will never rise above the level of being an 'unconscious Christian', to his own loss and the loss of the Christian fellowship which we call the Church.

This country, at least, has many thousands of such unconscious Christians. These men and women need to be told that what they are following, often spasmodically, is indeed ultimate reality and has been focused for us all in the recorded life of Jesus Christ.

They already know something of love, but the garbled version of the gospel which they hear from certain high-pressure evangelists does nothing to associate in their minds the ideas of 'love' and of 'God'.

How early Paul saw the full truth we do not precisely know, but certainly in 1 Corinthians 13, he has reached a point of insight which is quite miraculous in a man with his training and background.

He sees now with the utmost clarity that whatever tremendous and impressive things he may accomplish, however wide and deep his knowledge, however strong his faith, if he has no love, he amounts to nothing at all.

✤

22 May

THE SHELF

I think of the many unsolved problems and puzzles of this life.

It is true that, by the same Spirit, we are given an insight and an understanding into God's ways and workings that we should never have possessed by ourselves. But it is still true that life often baffles and perplexes us, and, if you will not think me too childish, what I think we need is a good solid 'shelf' on which such things may be left until the time comes for us to know even as we are known.

The 'shelf' is, of course, God himself. When we are able to cast all our care upon him, I feel our care may rightly include our unsolved problems and difficulties.

The sensitive man who lives this life without God must bear the burden, for he thinks and feels all the tragedies of this life by himself and, not infrequently, he breaks under the strain. But the Christian is not required to solve every problem and explain every difficulty and interpret every tragedy. It is not that he is excused from using his intelligence, his sympathy and his insight. It is simply that where he is completely baffled, he can trust.

He knows the kind of God who is his Father.

He knows too that, in the end, his Father will do all things well.

✤

23 May

THE BATTLEGROUND

The moment we begin to attempt seriously (by that I do not mean solemnly) to follow Jesus Christ, we find a dead and depressing weight of opposition both within us and without us. It is depressing because it is not a violent hostility, but a soul-destroying apathy, aptly expressed by that truly horrifying expression, 'I couldn't care less'.

I say it is within us as well as without us because the fog of unbelief has seeped into many Christian lives and choked their joy and confidence. Even where the existence of a God is admitted, he is so often regarded as an absentee non-intervening power, so that much of the New Testament reads, even to the Christian, like a 'beautiful dream'.

This is where I believe we have got to do battle, and do battle first with that refusal to believe which has come to live within our hearts. Looking aside for a moment from the revealed Word of God, can we not see the utter absurdity of God's expecting us, impotent beings, to live as his sons, his representatives, his ambassadors, unless he guarantees and provides constantly the power to enable us so to believe and so to behave? If Christianity is to be of any use at all in the redemption of the world, it *must* be a super-natural quality of life, invading ordinary human life from within. God does as he must, pour into human lives those extra qualities which the sons of God need for their living:

'Strengthened with all might according to his glorious power' (Colossians 1:11).

'Filled with the knowledge of God' (Colossians 1:9).

'Able to withstand the evil day' (Ephesians 6:13).

'Filled with all the fullness of God' (Ephesians 3:19).

'Blameless and harmless, the sons of God' (Philippians 2:15).

'Kept by the power of God' (1 Peter 1:5).

Those are only a few of the bits of the evidence, taken at random from his Word.

✛

24 May

GOD IS PRESENT

The presence of God is a fact of life. St Paul rightly said of God, 'in whom we live and move and have our being'. Jesus said, 'The Kingdom of God is within you.'

We may, by defying the purpose of God, insulate ourselves from that presence.

We may, by unrepented sin, cut off the sense of God because we are clouded by a sense of guilt.

We may, through no fault of our own, be unable to sense the God who is all about us.

But the fact remains that he is with us all the time.

The Psalmist long ago realized this 'inescapableness' of God when he wrote, 'Whither shall I go from thy spirit or whither shall I flee from thy presence? If I ascend up into heaven, thou art there; if I make my bed in hell, thou art there also' (Psalm 139:7–8).

We can make the most of our sense of the presence of God:

- by making sure that we are proceeding along the path of God's will for us;
- by using our imagination deliberately to remind ourselves that, though we do not deserve it, the Spirit of God is continually with us;
- by deliberately making special times in our lives, in private as well as in public, when we consciously recollect the presence of God.

That is why such things as a 'quiet time' are so valuable in our private lives and Holy Communion so valuable when we meet together in fellowship.

25 May

OUR DESTINY

Never mind about the forms of the myths which, we are told, are all that 'religion' has ever been. The dragons and the monsters may never have been real, but the malignant diabolical powers which they stand for are as alive and virulent as ever.

Whether you talk of God or Devil, you are bound to use picture-language, but that does not mean that behind the 'pictures' the truth is no longer true.

Jesus was never a shepherd but he can be a Shepherd in our pastoral needs in this age. He was never a door. But he is a true opening to the knowing of God and I have hundreds of letters to prove it.

We who teach or preach or speak or write must renew the vision. We must recover the dimension of the spiritual and the timeless, or people will inevitably lower their standards and destroy each other.

This naturally does not matter much to the Communist or even to the humanist-atheist; for to them all life ends in physical death anyway. But to those of us who know in our hearts that our destiny is far higher than at present any words can even attempt to express, we must do all we can, with the help of the unseen Spirit, to halt this disintegration, and reinstate honour, respect, and faith both for God and fellow man.

❖

26 May

THE NEW OPIUM OF THE PEOPLE

The attack on the only faith worth holding is being made by subtle means. The 'clevers' in their ivory towers nibble away at the moral certainties until un-clever man is no longer sure of what is right and what is wrong. He has been 'conned' into the belief that God is dead. He dare not criticize what is lewd, salacious and corrupting for fear of being called a prude. He scarcely dares to lift a finger to ease men's burdens for he will be scorned as a 'do-gooder'.

The ancient Hebrew book of Proverbs says, 'where there is no vision, the people cast off restraint' (Proverbs 29:18, JB). This is happening every day before our eyes. It is materialistic humanism and not religion which today is 'the opium of the people'.

Deprive mankind of ultimate authority and of the whole dimension of the spiritual and he is reduced indeed—a creature lacking any real significance and stripped of any ideals worth striving for, or victories worth winning.

He falls to polluting himself and his environment both physically and morally, and does not know how to stop.

❖

27 May

A CAUSE REMAINS

We can do little or nothing about the basic terms on which we live life. It is only after acceptance of these terms that we can do something constructive and practical.

The countries of the free world have suffered patiently the cults of 'angry young men' or their equivalents. More serious attention would be deserved by the outbursts against 'things as they are' if the rebels themselves would do something more than denounce and destroy.

They claim that there are no causes left to live and die for, but I have yet to hear of an angry young man dedicating his life to the cure of leprosy, to the care of crippled children or the spreading of medical knowledge in newly awakening continents, to name but a few of the worthwhile human causes.

They cry that they have nothing in which to put their faith, but have they seriously considered the claims of true Christianity?

If one looks upon human life as a challenge to courage, compassion and charity, the anger could be readily transformed into worthwhile energy, the frustration be resolved and the self-pity be forgotten.

❖

28 May

LIFE-ENHANCING

Christianity is an invitation to true living, and its truth is only endorsed by actual experience.

When a man becomes a committed Christian he sooner or later sees the falsity, the illusions, and the limitations of the humanist geocentric way of thinking. He becomes (sometimes suddenly, but more often gradually) aware of a greatly enhanced meaning in life and of a greatly heightened personal responsibility.

Beneath the surface of things as they seem to be, he can discern a kind of cosmic conflict in which he is now personally and consciously involved.

He has ceased to be a spectator or a commentator and a certain small part of the battlefield is his alone.

He also becomes aware, as probably never before, of the forces ranged against him.

❖

29 May

THE TRUTH MATTERS

Although I believe in the true inspiration of the New Testament and its obvious power to change human lives in this or any other country, I make it clear that I cannot possibly hold the extreme 'fundamentalist' position of so-called 'verbal inspiration'.

This theory is bound to break down sooner or later in the world of translation.

You cannot talk to tribes who live without ever seeing navigable water of our possessing an 'anchor for the soul'.

You cannot speak to the Eskimos of 'the Lamb of God which taketh away the sin of the world', or of Christ being 'the true Vine' and of us, his disciples, as 'the branches'!

Such examples could, literally, be multiplied many thousands of times. Yet I have found, when addressing meetings in this country and in America, that there still survives a minority who passionately believe in verbal inspiration. It appears that they have never seriously thought that there are millions for whom Christ died who would find a word-for-word translation of the New Testament, even if it were possible, frequently meaningless.

Any man who has sense as well as faith is bound to conclude that it is the *truths* which are inspired and not the words which are merely the vehicles of truth.

✤

30 May

999

People have got some very odd ideas about God! Somehow or other, although they have grown up in a dozen other ways and become very skilled in their own line, where God is concerned they still hold on to ideas they had when they were little children. They see him as either a vague benevolence 'above the bright blue sky' or else some sort of celestial policeman waiting to pounce on you if you put a foot wrong. Or perhaps he is just the heavenly 999 that you dial in an emergency —the prayer you make when you are really up against it!

These childish notions of God are not the slightest use in the real business of living. They are moreover contrary to the teaching of Christ.

The whole point of Christianity is that God has been here, on this planet.

He became a Man in the person of Jesus Christ.

He lived life on ordinary human terms and he knew the meaning of hard work, of sorrow and disappointment and fear and temptation.

In the end the forces of evil closed in on him and killed him, publicly and painfully.

It was a horrible tragedy and his friends thought it was the end, the end of the finest man who ever lived.

But it was not the end. It was shown that he was alive, that he had conquered death just as he said he would.

And he promised that he would be with those who believed in him till the end of the world.

✤

31 May

STRANGERS AND PILGRIMS

For all we know, we may be near the end of all things. You simply cannot read the New Testament fairly and come to the conclusion that the world is going to become better and better, happier and happier, until at last God congratulates mankind on the splendid job they have made of it! Quite the contrary is true. Not only Jesus, but Paul, Peter, John and the rest never seriously considered human perfectibility in the short span of earthly life.

This is the preparation, the training-ground, the place where God begins his work of making us into what he wants us to be.

But it is not our home.

We are warned again and again not to value this world as a permanency. Neither our security nor our true wealth is rooted in this passing life. We are strangers and pilgrims and, while we are under the pressure of love to do all that we can to help our fellows, we should not expect a world which is largely God-resisting to become some earthly paradise.

All this may sound unbearably old-fashioned, but this is the view of the New Testament as a whole.

Plant your feet firmly therefore within the freedom that Christ has won for us, and do not let yourselves be caught again in the shackles of slavery... If you try to be justified by the law you automatically cut yourself off from the power of Christ, you put yourself outside the range of his grace. For it is by faith that we await in his Spirit the righteousness we hope to see... Here is my advice. Live your whole life in the Spirit and you will not satisfy the desires of your lower nature.

GALATIANS 5:1, 4–5, 16

June

The Spirit, however, produces in human life fruits such as these: love, joy, peace, patience, kindness, generosity, fidelity, tolerance and self-control.

GALATIANS 5:22–23

1 June

THE WHOLE CHURCH

The way of recovery for modern man undoubtedly lies through the recovery of the *whole* Christian Church.

Throughout the centuries there has been no deep and lasting revitalization of the Christian religion unless the rekindled faith has been welded into the life of the existing Church. Enthusiastic 'splinter-groups' and separatist movements may blaze impressively for a time, but if the new life is to be effectual, it must flow into the body of believers already existing, however moribund and defeated they may appear to have become.

It is not so much the isolated Christian as a purified and refreshed fellowship, which will be the effective witness to a largely despairing world.

2 June

GOD'S AMBITION

Our generation needs a living God.

Because we believe in and have some conception of the necessity for atonement, we are apt to give the impression that God is preoccupied with sin or at least with moral welfare. But surely God's real 'ambition', if I may use such a word, is rather different. His purpose is, cost what it may, 'to bring many sons to glory'. And that purpose is not in the least altered or modified by contemporary pressures.

We who are human beings can very easily get hot under the collar at the decline in moral standards, the desecration of the Lord's day and a host of other things which are merely symptoms of dis-ease. What has really happened is that the old, somewhat primitive sanctions and restrictions of the God of Queen Victoria have been cast aside. Modern life has however obscured the 'bigness' of the life and the purpose of God.

It is our task to present the eternal but contemporary God, who was, and is, 'in Christ reconciling the world to himself, not imputing their trespasses to them' (2 Corinthians 5:19).

3 June

THE HEALING SPIRIT

I believe the recovery of real religion to be essential to the well-being of modern humanity. But, alas, the very word 'religion' has the wrong associations for many. They think of Puritanism, of churchiness, of spiritual restriction, of taboos, of dreary church services and senti-mental hymns, of pious legend, of traditional thinking, of the attempt to squeeze all truth into a narrow religious mould, of the inefficiency and blindness of some churches, of the hypocrites who profess one thing and obviously believe another, of blind faith with its fear of true knowledge, of the pride of those who believe that they alone hold the truth—and so on, *ad nauseam*.

What I am pleading for when I urge a return to real religion, is something quite different. It must mean a willing adjustment to our situation as human beings in the whole creation, and that must mean *accepting a relationship not only with other human beings but with the Spirit behind the whole scheme*.

If there is no restoring force, no healing and rehabilitating Spirit, no extra-human source of goodness and compassion, then many of us are indeed undone.

If *I* did not know that there was such restoration and reinforcement, that there are such springs which can be tapped by human beings, *I* should be lost.

✤

4 June

THE SLAVE OF JESUS

We all know how hard it is to admit that we are wrong, but it is difficult even to begin to imagine the inward cost to a proud and privileged Pharisee in becoming a follower, indeed, as he says again and again, a slave of Jesus Christ.

When Saul of Tarsus was converted to the new faith, the vision of the risen Christ was sudden and unexpected, but we may be sure that Saul, now Paul, with his strict pharisaic training, his sensitivity and high intelligence must have undergone prolonged agonies of mind and spirit in accepting the changes.

For Saul to have become Paul must have been very painful.

5 June

TOWARD SENSE

Christianity, which is a solid, down-to-earth, common-sense way of living, begins with faith, that is, believing that the eternal God whose 'size' and power and wisdom science is more and more uncovering, did, as a matter of sheer historical fact, enter this world over nineteen hundred years ago in the person of a human baby.

It takes faith to believe that, as well as a lot of honest sweat in reading the records (in the Gospels of your New Testament) of what that baby said and did when he grew up to be a man. But millions of people have found that, when they believe his claim to be God in human form, life begins to make sense.

God is then no longer a faraway power, securely insulated from all the pain and tragedy of this world, watching us men like ants in an ant-heap.

He is the God who became one of us.

6 June

WORSHIP

Everybody worships something or somebody. It may be a film star, a footballer, a radio personality, a writer, a painter or a ballerina. It may even be, for some poor lonely soul, the cat or the canary. But to all ordinary people there is something or somebody that calls out respect, admiration, love, and possibly wonder or even awe.

That is worship.

Listen to the crowd on the football ground, cheering and yelling—and giving advice. It is not merely the result of the match, but the physical fitness, the skill and dash of the team that is exciting admiration and enthusiasm and affection.

Listen to the applause after a concert at the Albert Hall. You can almost feel the waves of admiration and gratitude and even love that flow towards those who have brought beauty and delight to the audience.

We may think that worship is often misdirected, or that the objects of people's worship are not worth the love and devotion given to them, but we cannot say that people do not worship!

What we can say is that most people do not see any connection between the love and admiration and enthusiasm that they pour out for their favourite things or people and what Christians call 'worshipping God'.

✤

7 June

AN INSTINCT PRESERVED

At present the religious instinct, which I believe to exist in every man, is being perverted. All men naturally worship someone or something (as we noted yesterday), but in the commonly assumed absence of God, this worship is given, as I said in yesterday's 'thought', almost wholly to such things as success, sport, the heroes or heroines of the fantasy-world of the screen or stage, or to the mysteries of science.

Such a superstition as astrology may flourish as a substitute religion for the ignorant, while some fancy version of an Eastern religion may attract the intellectual agnostic. But perversions of the instinct to worship God do not in the long run rescue man either from his own solitariness or from the closed-system of materialism.

The way out, paradoxically enough, lies in no form of uncommitted escapism, but in a closer commitment to life. Christianity shows the way to such closer commitment; it does not merely restore a man's faith in God but inevitably involves him in compassion and service.

This is both the strength and the difficulty about the Christian way of life. Other methods may give 'religious' experiences, but only Christianity insists that the life of the spirit must be expressed within the terms of the present human predicament.

That is why only Christianity can fully satisfy the desire to worship and the desire to serve.

8 June

'COME AND WORSHIP'

In the palmy days when I enjoyed the services of two first-class curates and an excellent lay-reader, there were times when I was able to attend services at my own church by slipping quietly into the back pew.

I did this, in the first instance, with a critical professional eye and ear, so that our worship might be of the best possible quality. But, rather to my surprise, I found myself aware of an almost indescribable feeling among the congregation, which I can only describe as a wistful hunger to know more of God.

In the parish of which I am speaking, I should say that very few went to church out of mere habit or duty, and certainly none went because it was 'the thing to do' (it wasn't!).

These people came to worship and to pray, but most of all (or so was my strong feeling) to hear more and learn more of the love of God.

9 June

THEY WANT TO KNOW...

Like anyone else who cares for the souls of men, I was moved almost to tears by the quiet receptiveness of ordinary people in church. For in the house of God, they have temporarily laid aside mundane pressures and responsibilities. For the time being at least they are set free from the rat-race of competition and from the need to keep up appearances.

In a sense they are naked and vulnerable. More than a little puzzled, sometimes more than a little battered by life's problems, they are seeking news about God.

It is monstrous for the preacher to offer such people a theological digest on the latest book on demythologizing the Gospels. Neither have they come to church to hear the preacher thundering against the sins of those who are not within earshot.

They simply want to know about God.

They want to hear the Good News.

May they always be given it!

10 June

LOYALTIES

Amid all the conflicts of loyalties—to one's friends, to parents, to one's employer, to one's own 'principles'—the overriding loyalty must always be the loyalty to God himself. To have made the great decision to follow the living Christ at all costs means that a number of lesser decisions have been automatically made.

An enormous amount of human suffering and misery is caused every day simply because men and women have never made any such decision. They are at the mercy of their own whims and desires, and those of other people. Their lives are chaotic because they have never been aligned with any great purpose.

Discarded loyalties and faith thrown overboard may look like gestures of freedom at the time.

But look around and see what happens in the years that follow to the people who despise faith and loyalty.

11 June

COMPETITIONS IN GOODNESS

There is a basic misconception held by a great many people outside the Christian Church.

It is commonly supposed that, in the religious view, life is primarily a kind of competition in goodness and morality! Consequently, the agnostic who can, and frequently does say, 'I am as good as so-and-so who goes to church,' feels that he has given a final and unanswerable reply to the whole Christian position!

True Christianity has, however, never taught that life is primarily a kind of competition in goodness. Most Christians today are 'in the Church', because they have felt the need for God and for co-operating with what they know of his purpose.

There probably were times in the history of the Christian Church in this country when some churchgoing Christians would look upon themselves as 'superior' to those outside the Church. But to imagine that such is the common attitude today would be laughable if it were not a tragic part of the misunderstanding between the worlds of faith and unfaith.

✣

12 June

INTELLECTUAL SNOBBERY

I remember a former high dignitary of the Church of England who was presented with a fountain-pen. But he never used it, on the simple grounds that 'he did not understand mechanical things'!

I cannot see why the artist should despise the engineer or the engineer the artist, and I have little patience for artists or intellectuals of one sort or another who dismiss a scientific device, which has taken years of patience to perfect, as a mere gadget.

Those who make it their proud boast that they 'don't know the first thing about electricity and couldn't even mend a fuse' or, when referring to their car, say, 'I haven't the remotest idea what goes on under the bonnet, I just drive the thing', are to my mind guilty of a quite unpardonable conceit. It would not take them long to understand at least the elementary principles of those things which they affect to despise, and even to have some clue to the rudiments might give them an inkling into the enormous skill, patience and ingenuity which lie behind the practical application of physical science.

Those who loudly deplore the intrusion of 'science' into our private lives and speak nostalgically of the past would be among the first to complain if they were deprived of the convenience of electric light, the telephone or the motor car!

✣

13 June

DIAGNOSIS AND PRESCRIPTION

David Grayson, the American essayist, was seriously ill and spent some months in hospital. He reflected on that experience in a charming and rewarding little book called *Adventures in Solitude*. He writes:

As I thought during those long days, it seemed to me that the hospital cherishes a spirit, or an attitude, that the Church sadly lacks. I felt in it a respect for the human body and for human life beyond that in the Church, as it stands today, for the spirit of man.

The hospital diagnoses before it prescribes; the Church prescribes before it diagnoses. The physician stands humble before the human body, studies it, doubts about it, wonders at it; labours to fit his remedies to the exact disease. Is there in any church an equivalent humility in the presence of the spirit of man? Is the priest willing to inquire and doubt and wonder? Does he know before he tries to cure? Must the Church cultivate certainty lest knowledge turn and rend it?

The words, 'the Church prescribes before it diagnoses' have haunted me. It is easy to leap hotly to the defence of the Church and say that, after all, she holds a divine prescription as well as a divine diagnosis. That is true, but the souls of men are delicate and complex affairs and their spiritual needs are never going to be met by mass prescription.

The good priest approaches human beings with exactly that humility and willingness to learn that David Grayson here describes.

✛

14 June

FAMILIARITY

Most practising Christians have got beyond feeling that God must be addressed in Elizabethan English in deference to His Majesty, but there still lingers on an idea that we must be spiritually 'dressed in our best' as we approach him.

I am far from suggesting that we should ever treat the awe-inspiring mystery of God with over-familiarity. Yet we know perfectly well, on the authority of Christ, that he is our heavenly Father and our common sense tells us that, although he respects our individuality and our privacy, yet everything about us is quite open to his eyes.

We are not addressing some super-earthly King, some magnified Boss. We are not even addressing a purified and enlarged image of our own earthly fathers.

We are opening our hearts to love.

We need have no fears, no reticences, and no pretences.

15 June

IN THE DARK

Some people have it. Some don't. It depends on health, circumstances and all sorts of other things. I mean the experience of having to go on living when, for the time being at least, all the joy and colour has gone out of life, and even the sense of God has disappeared.

It is a common happening for most of us, for brief intervals. Usually a good night's rest or a short holiday restores things to normal. But there are thousands of men and women who have to experience this sense of darkness and solitariness for months on end.

It can be a tough test of character and of faith in God.

It is a test because it is so easy to give up. Life is full of people who 'used to believe'. But because things turned out darker and tougher than they supposed, they have decided that 'there can't be a God to let things like that happen'.

But 'things like that' have always happened, to all sorts of people; even to Christ. We simply do not know *why* life should, apparently, be so easy for one and so heartbreakingly difficult for another.

Let's not pretend. No one *likes* pain of difficulty or this sense of darkness and being alone. But if we can accept it as part of life and hold on to the God who, apparently, isn't there, we shall eventually emerge toughened and strenghened.

16 June

INNER CERTAINTY

I believe inner certainty is a possibility and a necessity for us all in uncertain days.

Here are some of my reasons:

1. Our faith rests not upon a dialectic argument or a beautiful myth, but on a fact of history.
2. The promise of Christ who is 'the same yesterday, today and for ever' was to be with us always 'even unto the end of the world'. I feel sure therefore that the certainty of Christ was not intended simply to be a phenomenon of the first century but was to be the prerogative of the Church on earth as long as that Church exists.
3. Though I am not a fundamentalist in the narrow sense of that term, my close study of the New Testament has convinced me of the very real inspiration, not only of the Gospels but also of the Epistles. Nothing short of the direct inspiration of God can, for example, explain the breathtaking assurances of St Paul and St John.

These men are not making up a case.

They are stating facts.

If these facts about God were true nineteen hundred years ago, *they are true now*, for God does not change however much our scene may shift.

These men were certain.

Why should we not be certain too?

17 June

JESUS THE DISTURBER

H.G. Wells was not a Christian but he wrote in his *History of the World*:

Jesus appeared in Judea in the reign of Tiberius Caesar… a very definite personality. One is obliged to say: 'Here was a man'. This could not have been invented. He was like some terrible moral huntsman digging mankind out of the snug burrows in which they had lived hitherto. For to take him seriously was to enter upon a strange and alarming life, to abandon habits, to control instincts and impulses and to essay an incredible happiness.

Jesus is far more than a 'terrible moral huntsman', but the records of the New Testament, seriously read, do leave people profoundly disturbed.

You can read a much more detailed and intimate account of the thoughts and teachings of Marcus Aurelius who lived at roughly the same time. But, although many have admired him, his influence upon human life is not one ten-millionth part of that of the one of whom, alas, we know so little.

✣

18 June

WHERE THE TREASURE IS

English people are unfairly suspicious of their emotions. We link emotion with the sentimental, the weak and the unmanly, and it has become second nature to us to repress outward signs of emotion.

However desirable that may be as a national trait, it is silly to act as if reason was a thing to be trusted and the emotions were purely a set of savage animals to be kept under strict control. For all that happens is that emotions which are never recognized, remain underdeveloped and are accordingly distrusted. If, on the other hand, they are frankly recognized as the great driving forces of life without there having to be any untoward display of emotionalism, our lives would be fuller and richer.

The emotions can be trained just as the intellect can. We spend years training our minds but we spend very little on training the emotions.

The result of all this is clear. We have men and women trained in mind but with the emotional life of savages. The fruit of their intellect is therefore shown in the production of machines for destroying each other with the maximum of pain and the minimum of trouble.

Jesus was wise when he founded his religion and his kingdom on a change in the emotional life.

For if that can be changed, then human behaviour is automatically changed.

'Where your treasure is, there shall your heart be also' (Matthew 6:21).

❖

19 June

IN HEART AND MIND

Our habit of repressing all the softer emotions may lead that side of our nature to express itself in religion! I know, for instance, an exceedingly hard-boiled scout troop in south-east London, which invariably chooses the sloppiest and most sentimental hymns to accompany their closing prayers.

It is plain that they are finding in their religion the tenderness which the rest of their activities are constantly repressing. This means in effect that 'gentle Jesus meek and mild' is taking the place of the mother's arms that part of their nature still remembers. This means that in latter years when they 'put away childish things', they will tend to relegate religion to the soft and childish past, and feel that a grown-up person has no need for anything so sentimental.

The remedy for this is two-fold:

- Not to hold up for admiration an artificially tough and hearty attitude to life, but to show that the tender side of life, the love and beauty, family affection, the love of pets, and so on, are equally a natural part of life.
- To give the Christian religion a respectable place in young people's minds as well as in their hearts, so that while their emotional life is changing, they will have an intellectual hold upon the truth.

140

20 June

SPEAK OUT!

When the Christian looks at 'the news', he usually sees a very different spirit from that of Christ. He reads of fear, oppression, exploitation, cruelty, bad faith and the whole tragic tale of man's inhumanity to man. Quite rightly he feels that he cannot be silent. He must protest where and when he can.

Should he?

It is unrealistic for Christians to legislate for non-Christians. The Christian may, and indeed must, protest at what he knows is wrong, but he must at all times realize that people cannot be *made* good, or kind, or loving, or understanding, by force of law. Moreover, he will be wise to avoid hasty comment on issues where honest political opinion is divided, and where even good Christian men hold opposing views.

Where he must *not* be silent is where human rights, human liberties and human dignity are concerned.

Speak out, whatever the cost and whatever the consequences!

21 June

DOING GOOD

It seems extraordinary that our society has coined the name 'do-gooder' to use as a term of contempt! To do good can surely be nothing *but* good, and deserves to be appreciated, if not openly praised. After all, was it not said of Jesus that 'he went about doing good'?

If, of course, we are simply showing off our superior morality or prosperity, we are not better than the Lady Bountifuls of days gone by, who out of their vast riches gave bread and soup to the deserving poor. That said, it must be God's will that we 'do good'.

People are quick to resent being patronized or being made to feel inferior. Unless our service to other people springs from true concern and compassion for them, we can never rise above the level of the 'do-gooder'. But let us not be discouraged. Many people have found that, if they begin to give themselves for others, their love and concern deepens. The tiny spark of compassion becomes a steady-burning flame.

Jesus is our supreme example here. He genuinely loved people, and whether he was criticized for keeping dubious company ('a friend of publicans and sinners'), or for being too fond of the good things of life ('a wine-bibber and a gluttonous man'), he went steadily on, bringing health and hope by means of self-giving love, doing good.

If we are living close to Jesus, it will not really matter if the careless do refer to us as mere 'do-gooders'.

✢

22 June

THE SOFTER SIDE

Once, when I was a schoolmaster, I was asked on a Good Friday morning by a rather harassed headmaster to take a class which had been left unattended through the illness of one of the staff.

'I do not mind what you do with them as long as you keep them quiet for the next forty minutes,' he said.

As it was Good Friday, I thought I would read them something appropriate, and I read from Paterson Smyth's *Life of Christ*, the story of the first Good Friday.

These boys, though they were mostly children of well-to-do parents, were in almost complete ignorance of the Christian religion. Yet although I read that chapter in a matter-of-fact voice, you could have heard a pin drop throughout that period. There were even tears in the eyes of some of the 'hardest nuts'.

I mention this because of the lesson it taught me, namely that we must not judge boys by outward appearances only. There is, of course, a place for noisiness and toughness, but there is also in the plastic growing material that we are dealing with, a gentler, softer side. It may often be hidden but is certainly there.

❖

23 June

'QUIT YOU LIKE MEN!'

For far too long people have thought that the Christian Church was meant chiefly for women and children; that real men had finished with such 'childish things'. Turn back then to the New Testament, when the Church was courageous, gay, tough and vigorous and see how many men were in it and of it!

It is true that women feature quite prominently in the 'new society' that Christ founded. It is remarkable too that this fresh way of living obviously appealed to men of courage, intelligence and ability. Paul, himself no weakling, writes in one of the earliest New Testament letters, 'quit you *like men*, be strong' (1 Corinthians 16:13).

What has gone wrong? Have we, the preachers and ministers, emphasized the wrong things? Have we been offering comfort, consolation and support only? These things *are* part of the Christian gospel, but only a part. Christ himself could be infinitely tender, but he could also be amazingly tough.

I read somewhere that '*Christ has no use for the weak*'. I blinked, and read again. The author continued: 'I did not say Christ had no *time* for the weak—he has all the time in the world. But he has no *use* for the weak in the building of his Kingdom.'

In other words Christ takes us, weak as we are, and makes us into strong builders of the Kingdom.

✣

24 June

THE UNCOMFORTABLE WORLD

It seems to me (and heaven knows one can observe this sort of spirit in oneself) that human beings are for ever trying to evade moral responsibility while God is eternally trying to make them accept it, and grow up to be his sons.

This move by human beings is a clever one. By identifying ourselves, in imagination of course, with 'the sinner', we feel we have proved our compassion, our reluctance to condemn and our 'understanding'. We have also relieved our personal sense of guilt by persuading ourselves that we are all in it together. At the same time, and in a much subtler way, we are condoning the evil in others as well as in ourselves. Before long we are saying, and probably believing, 'of course there is no such thing as *right* or *wrong*—it is all relative' (although what they are relative *to* is never clear).

Because of this tendency in human beings to evade moral responsibility (the method, but not the tendency changing with the generations), the world of the Bible is bound to be an uncomfortable world.

There God, not man, is master.

There God speaks.

Man, if he is wise, listens with humility.

✣

25 June

THE LEG WE NEED

If it is true that there are no such things as real moral standards, then it is simply a question of one man's opinion against another on any question. You can say that the Communist way of life, with its worship of the state, its secret police, its slave camps and all the rest seems wrong to you, but the Communist can equally well say that our way of life, with its freedom of speech, freedom of worship and all the other things we treasure seems wrong to him.

We may think it wrong to ill-treat animals, to exploit child labour and to keep women ignorant and uneducated. But there are plenty of places in the world where our attitude in these matters would be considered silly, weak and sentimental.

What we really need is to find a way of living which is applicable to all men, despite their differences of temperament and outlook. We cannot find that without bringing in God. For however passionately we may believe in the 'British way of life' or the 'American way of life', we cannot expect the Chinese or the Egyptians or the Indians, for example, to accept these ways just because we believe in them.

If, however, we can say that the way of living that we believe in, has behind it the authority of God himself who is the Father of all mankind, then we do have a leg on which to stand.

Have we got that?

✣

26 June

'ONE MAN'S MEAT...'

It is extraordinary how different people are. One man likes jazz and pop, another listens to nothing but Radio 3. One man's idea of recreation is rock-climbing and another man's playing snooker. There is just no accounting for tastes!

Cross over into another country, say, France or Italy or the United States of America, and you get bigger differences still. Customs, conventions, habits of thought and behaviour vary tremendously from place to place, so that we may be quite shocked at something which 'foreigners' think quite normal and natural, while they are equally shocked at what appears to us quite innocent and ordinary.

Now that men are getting to know the world better and are seeing how differently other people live, we sometimes get people saying that there isn't any real *right and wrong*. It is only a question of upbringing or the country or century in which you happen to live.

Obviously this suits some people ideally! They can do just what they like. If anyone objects, they can simply say that they are merely rejecting artificial standards, the conventional morality of the day, and so on.

This idea has seeped through into popular thinking and accounts for quite a lot of the decline in the standards of morality.

If there are no real standards for human living, then any man can construct his own code of behaviour, or indeed dispense with a code at all.

❖

27 June

'CHOOSE YOU, THIS DAY'

If we believe that Jesus Christ was not merely the best man that ever lived but God revealing himself in human form, then we have the authority for which we are looking. For he came not only to show the character of God but to outline the kind of behaviour which leads to happy and constructive human living. Indeed, if we think about it, we can see that all that is best in our national tradition, justice, honesty, morality, and consideration for the underdog, are really the fruit in national life of many centuries of Christian faith.

The trouble today is that so many people in this country are leading kindly decent lives, treating others as they would like to be treated themselves, *without knowing why*. They are, so to speak, living on the spiritual capital of the past, and they are not adding to the strength of the Christian tradition by any faith of their own.

You may be one of those people. *You* believe certain things are 'decent' and right, but do *you* know why?

It is not really enough to say that you *feel* that they are right, because other countries, with other customs and traditions, may not share your feeling at all. The only way out of complete chaos, where it is always going to be one man's opinion against another's, is for you to accept the authority of God as shown by Christ.

In a topsy-turvy world, we have to make a choice.

It can only be faith in our own opinions or faith in the moral laws of God.

'Choose you this day...'

✢

28 June

THE SPEARHEAD

The strategy of Christ was to win the loyalty of the few who would honestly respond to the new way of living. They would be the pioneers of the new order, the spearhead of advance against the massed ignorance, selfishness, evil, 'play-acting', and apathy of the majority of the human race.

The goal which was set before them, for which they were to work and pray—and if need be, suffer and die—was the building of a new Kingdom of inner supreme loyalty, the Kingdom of God. This was to transcend every barrier of race and frontier and—and this is important—of time and space as well.

The 'Church', which became the name of the spearhead, has been, and is, open to a good deal of criticism, but it has made a great deal of hard-won progress. It is, at any rate, trying to carry out the divine plan, and in so far as it is working along the lines of real truth and real love it cannot, of course, fail—any more than God can cease to exist.

29 June

SENT TO TRY US

Probably not very many who use this everyday expression, take it seriously. But suppose it is true?

The New Testament certainly supports this view—that the 'trying' or 'testing' of our faith and courage is an essential part of our growth as sons of God.

Jesus himself was severely tried and tested in the forty days which the season of Lent represents. 'He was', we are told by the author of the Epistle to the Hebrews, 'in all things tempted (that is tested or tried) like as we are'. And every true follower of his, in every century, has had his faith tested, sometimes severely and often for a long time.

To know that all our fellow Christians are subjected to temptations and trials may sometimes support and strengthen us. But possibly the thing that makes us resentful is the word in the saying 'sent'. It conjures up a picture of some far away Father-figure in heaven doling out to us, poor struggling humans, all kinds of troubles and disasters while he himself remains aloof.

This is certainly not Christian teaching. Pain, suffering, trial and testing are part of the stuff of life itself and Jesus neither expected for himself, nor promised to his followers, any immunity from them.

But he did promise to be with them when it all happened.

30 June

UNCONQUERABLE

Jesus Christ himself began the vast project of establishing the Kingdom of God upon earth by calling together a handful of men.

Before his own departure from the visible human scene, he entrusted to these few the awe-inspiring task of telling the world about God and his Kingdom. He promised them supra-natural power, wisdom and love.

The Acts of the Apostles shows how this close-knit fellowship set out with joyful and hopeful audacity to build the Kingdom of Light in the stygian darkness of the pagan world.

These early Christians were held together by their common love for their Lord and his purpose, by their worship and their prayer. Violent persecution, public torture, social ostracism and dreadful forms of death could neither quench the fire nor defeat the purpose of the young Church.

The movement proved unconquerable and still proves unconquerable.

Because its unseen roots are in the eternal God.

✣

Men have different gifts, but it is the same Sprit who gives them. There are different ways of serving God, but it is the same Lord who is served. God works through different men in different ways, but it is the same God who achieves his purpose through them all. The Spirit openly makes his gift to each man, so that he may use it for the common good. One man's gift by the Spirit is to speak with wisdom, another's to speak with knowledge. The same Spirit gives to another man faith, to another the ability to heal, to another the use of spiritual powers. The same Spirit gives to another man the gift of preaching the word of God, to another the ability to discriminate in spiritual matters, to another speech in different tongues and to yet another the power to interpret the tongues. Behind all these gifts is the operation of the same Spirit, who distributes to each individual man, as he wills.

1 CORINTHIANS 12:4–11

July

I rely on this saying: If we died with him, we shall also live with him: if we endure we shall also reign with him. If we deny him, he will also deny us: yet if we are faithless he always remains faithful. He cannot deny his own nature.

Remind your people of things like this, and tell them as before God not to fight wordy battles, which help no one and may undermine the faith of those who hear them.

2 TIMOTHY 2:11–14

✣

1 July

RELAX!

Everybody needs to relax at some time or another. Any doctor would tell you that to be able to relax your body and your mind completely is wonderfully refreshing to the whole system.

But quite a lot of people, if the truth were told, find it very difficult to relax inside themselves.

There is nothing new about this problem of relaxation, and the religion of Jesus Christ offers a practical and realistic way out. It diagnoses the trouble, and gives the solution, rather like this (I give you rule no. 1 today):

Most people are not at peace with God or with their fellow men. Since none of us can undo the past, *the Christian faith prescribes accepting the forgiveness of God and living in love and charity with our neighbours.*

This may mean a certain amount of apology and admitting that we were wrong, but it is well worth the pain and effort.

2 July

RULES FOR RELAXATION

Here are more of the rules of relaxation:

The Christian faith recognizes that human beings have a conflict within themselves, and it prescribes *the accepting of God's own Spirit into our own personalities* so that what we sometimes call our better self is enormously strengthened, and the 'worse self' loses its power.

The Christian faith prescribes *an attitude of faith rather than of fear towards life*. However much appearances may be against it, God is really and ultimately in charge. Consequently, once our personalities are honestly entrusted to God, we can be sure there is nothing in life or death that can alter the fact that our lives are lived 'in God'.

That makes for a deep inner peace.

Inward peace is not merely the absence of outward worry and strain. *What we need is a positive peace which will keep us calm and poised, even when outward things are dark and difficult.*

Here the Christian faith offers us a gift. Christ says, 'My peace I leave with you, my peace I give unto you'. Those who accept this gift find that they do experience, right inside themselves, 'the peace which passes understanding'.

These rules are not theoretical but intensely practical, as thousands have proved.

There is no real and deep relaxation outside the peace of God.

✤

3 July

HOLIDAYS

The real, refreshing holiday is the one in which we take things easily, enjoying the fact that we can lay aside our everyday responsibilities.

But there will be times, in a real holiday, when we can take a good, objective look at ourselves.

It may be in the quiet fields, by the riverbank or on the lonely cliff top that we think afresh about ourselves, about life and about God.

It is not really a waste of time to use a few hours of our holiday to think about the deeper side of our nature.

For real refreshment and real peace can only come from within oneself.

No one can maintain serenity in this modern bustling world unless the Kingdom of God is established in his own heart.

❖

4 July

BESIDE THE SEA

Most Englishmen take their holidays by the sea. Even though it means long traffic queues on the road, or a crowded journey in a stuffy train, millions feel that they must get to the sea somehow!

I have often wondered about this. Admittedly the air is fresher, though the old myth about the 'ozone' is no longer considered true.

I think there is a deeper reason. I think we all at heart love freedom.

The sea offers us a prospect that can never be a built-up area.

'The world is too much with us,' wrote the poet Wordsworth about 150 years ago—not that he ever had to work in a busy shop or noisy factory or cope with the complexities of any modern business! But his words are even more true today. Most people are caught up in the complicated business of earning a living, and for most of the year they are subjected to noise, stress, strain and anxiety.

To be beside the sea is not only to provide a breath of fresh air for the body but a draught of peace for the mind, a reminder that the feverish activity of human beings is not everything.

There is a hint of the everlasting in the vastness of the sea.

✤

5 July

GOD IS GREATER...

Like many others, I find myself something of a perfectionist. If we are not careful, this obsession for the perfect can make us arrogantly critical of other people, and, in certain moods, desperately critical of ourselves.

In this state of mind, it is not really that I cannot subscribe to the doctrine of the forgiveness of sins, but that the tyrannical super-Me condemns and has no mercy on myself.

John, in his wisdom, points out in these inspired words, that 'if our hearts condemn us, *God is greater* than our heart, and knoweth all things'.

This is a gentle but salutary rebuke to our assumption that we know better than God!

✤

6 July

TOWARDS THE MARK...

Jesus sometimes appears to say contradictory things.

'Be ye perfect as your heavenly Father is perfect,' he once said, and many with a perfectionist streak in them have worried over such a command. Yet it was also Jesus who said, 'Take my yoke upon you and learn of me; for my yoke is easy and my burden light.' Are we to regard the Christian religion as a rigid 100 per cent demand for perfection, or a process of learning where the 'burden' is suited to each man's capacity?

Surely the explanation is that while we cannot apply perfectionist standards to ourselves (we should go mad if we did!) our constant aim must be towards becoming perfect. We must accept and work to the best of our ability at the particular task God has set each one in the building of his kingdom.

St Paul wrote, 'not as though I had already attained or were already perfect, but... I press toward the mark for the prize of the high calling of God in Christ Jesus' (Philippians 3:14).

We are to be perfect, but not in a day.

God's aim is to make us all perfect, but the process may be a long one.

It may in fact extend far beyond this little life.

7 July

RIGHTEOUS ANGER

I do not write for scholars; they can look after themselves. For twenty-five years I have written for the ordinary man who is no theologian. Alas, today, he frequently gets the impression that the New Testament is no longer historically reliable.

What triggers off my anger (righteous, I trust) against some of our 'experts' is this.

A clergyman, old, retired, useless if you like, took his own life because his readings of the 'new theology' and even some pro-grammes on television, finally drove him, in his loneliness and ill-health, to conclude that his own life's work had been founded on a lie. He felt that these highly qualified writers and speakers must know so much more than he that they must be right.

Jesus Christ did not really rise from the dead and the New Testa-ment, on which he had based his life and ministry, was no more than a bundle of myths.

It was too much for him.

But I feel angry about it.

8 July

THE EXPERTS

I cannot forget Christ's stern words about 'causing one of his little ones to stumble', or Paul's warning about 'the weaker brother'. We who have grown into a strong and mature faith must surely regard it as part of our responsibility to do or say nothing which would undermine faith.

I believe this to be especially binding upon us in the fields of mass communication. What can profitably be discussed between men of many years' Christian experience may be quite unsuitable for a television programme, which may be seen by the weak, the fearful, the lonely and the dying.

I make no plea for obscurantism. Those who know me as a parish priest will agree that I have always taken the line that if the Christian faith can be destroyed by somebody or other's clever-clever talk, it cannot be basically very strong. But the broadcaster, and perhaps especially the solo television speaker, enjoys an almost *ex cathedra* position of non-contradiction.

I am convinced that he has no right to air his own doubts and fancies as though they were matters of agreed faith among Christians.

9 July

MY TESTIMONY

Some of the intellectuals (by no means all, thank God!) who write so cleverly and devastatingly about the Christian faith appear to have no personal knowledge of the living God. For they lack awe. They lack humility. They lack the responsibility which every Christian owes to his weaker brother. They make sure they are never made 'fools for

Christ's sake', however many people's faith they may undermine.

Few people have had such a close and constant contact with the New Testament as I have. Even fewer have taken the trouble to understand the business of 'communication'.

I say this in no spirit of conceit. It is a matter of simple fact. I therefore feel it is time someone, who has spent the best years of his life in studying both the New Testament and good modern communicative English, speaks out.

I do not care a rap what the *avant-garde* scholars say.

I do very much care what *God* says and does.

I therefore felt compelled to write *Ring of Truth*.

It is my testimony to the historicity and reliability of the New Testament.

✣

10 July

PICTURE-LANGUAGE

I must record my sense of injustice that the Christian religion should be singled out as a target for criticism because it uses, and is bound to use, 'picture-language'. We all do it every day of our lives, and we are none the worse for it.

No one blames the accountant for talking of a 'balance', the economist for speaking of 'frozen assets', the electronics engineer for talking of a magnetic 'field', the traffic controller for referring to a 'peak' period, the electrical engineer for speaking of 'load-shedding' or the town planner for talking of a 'bottleneck'. Not one of these words is literally true but they convey quickly, and pretty accurately, an idea which can be readily understood.

I cannot see why we, who accept hundreds of such usages in every-day speaking and writing, should decide that an expression such as 'seated at the right hand of the Father' is either literally true or totally false.

Because picture-language is sometimes used, it does not follow that the actual events are unhistorical or 'mythical'.

✣

11 July

EARLY WARNINGS

Most people who know the Bible at all know that prophecy does not necessarily mean foretelling the future, although it may well include it.

I have so far only made one excursion into the world of the Old Testament, but a close study of the prophets' messages shows that such men are primarily concerned to declare the 'word of the Lord'. They saw, sometimes with startling and heartbreaking clarity, what would be bound to happen if the nation continued on a course contrary to the will of the Lord.

The time-sense was temporarily suspended and there is a dramatic 'fore-shortening' of things which were to come.

More frequently than not, their vision was quite astonishingly accurate, even though twenty or a hundred years might elapse before what they foresaw came true.

Their messages were 'early warnings' rather than long-term threats.

Prophecy is not necessarily prediction.

For the warning contained in the vision might lead to a change of heart, and therefore of subsequent events.

✣

12 July

TRUE HUMANISM

As far as the records show, Jesus gave only one parable of the final judgment which all men face after the probation of this life.

The criterion is neither religion, nor orthodoxy, nor respectability, but the way in which man has treated man (Matthew 25:31–46).

In this altogether revolutionary way of looking at things, which is unique to Christianity, Jesus deliberately and precisely identifies man's treatment of himself with man's treatment of man.

Here surely is the true humanism.

Because God has become man, all men are at least potentially sons of God.

It automatically becomes a serious offence to injure or exploit other people, not because of some vague humanist values but because God has done man the unspeakable honour of identifying himself with the human race.

✦

13 July

DYNAMIC FOR LIVING

In countries of traditional Christian values which may well lead the world in matters of justice and liberty, it is very easy to underestimate the powers of evil. The issues are blurred, and the battle between good and evil is scarcely recognized by the majority of people.

We know nothing at first-hand of the cruelty of dictatorship. We rarely have had to suffer for our faith, if indeed we have one. But how much longer this atmosphere of comfortable apathy is going to last is anybody's guess. Already we have a generation growing up without moral standards, with no sense of purpose and with little, if any, concern for the enormous human problems which are coming to light all over the world.

Mere 'kindness', 'niceness', 'goodwill', or 'tolerance' are never going to supply a dynamic for living, a cause for which to live and die, or a purpose commanding a man's total dedication.

We who are older may have jogged along, content with those liberal humanist values left to us by preceding ages of faith. But nothing less than the recovery of real Christianity, with its ineradicable emphasis upon human compassion, and its inexorable insistence upon the transience of this world and the reality of eternity, will ever put back into the disillusioned the faith, hope, courage and gaiety which are the marks of a human being co-operating with his Creator.

✣

14 July

BEYOND OUR DREAMS

It is taken for granted in the recorded teaching of Jesus (and in the New Testament generally) that his life is lived against a background of what can literally be translated as 'the life of the ages'. The present business of living is merely a prelude, acted in the time-and-space set-up on this planet, to life in another dimension where present limitations do not obtain.

It is probably impossible to describe the next stage of existence in earthly terms, and it would be childish to take literally the picture-language of the New Testament writers who make some attempt to hint at its unimaginable splendours and possibilities. But the teaching of Christ is that the ultimate destiny of human beings, as far as we can at present comprehend it, is not extinction or absorption into the infinite, but the full development, the bringing to maturity, of sons of God.

For all we know, there lie ahead of us activities and responsibilities far beyond our present dreams, but at least it is clear that what we do in this present life is a significant factor in determining our status in the next.

✥

15 July

BREAD-AND-BUTTER STUFF

Real Christianity is good bread-and-butter stuff which nourishes men's souls by the worship of the true God and by the exercise of practical compassion.

But the fascination of modern technical advances in every department of our physical life has made us like spoiled children who long for sweets and more sweets, and have lost their stomach for truly nourishing food.

✥

16 July

LOVE'S VARIATIONS

As soon as we begin to study in earnest the recorded actions of Christ, we cannot help being struck by his extraordinary approach in dealing with different people. No rule of thumb is applied, but the purpose of constructive love is very flexible in the face of human complexities of character.

Thus, one person may immediately respond to the most uncompromising challenge, while another needs patient encouragement.

One is told that his life already approximates in pattern to what God is wanting him to be. Another may be told bluntly that despite all his religious profession he is at heart a 'child of evil'.

It is only when we detach 'texts of Scripture' that there are apparent contradictions in the sayings of Christ. Once we grasp the underlying principle of love in action touching human lives in various states of awareness and development, we can begin to understand why so many different things were said to so many different people.

17 July

AGGRESSIVE LOVE

It is true that Jesus offered no resistance to physical attacks against himself, but his love did not prevent him from using the most aggressive and blistering invective against those who thought they held a 'corner' in religion.

For all his loving-kindness, he did not hesitate to say that a man who led a little child astray would be better off dead.

He roundly declared that such notorious evil cities as Sodom and Gomorrah would fare better in the judgment than towns which rejected the living truth when it was before their eyes.

Jesus was no verbal sentimentalist. He was not prepared to gratify King Herod's whim to see him 'perform', but bluntly called him a fox.

He was moved to violent physical action by the combination of irreverence and black-marketeering which was corrupting what was meant to be the centre of worship—the Temple in Jerusalem.

We must not then over-simplify the issue and say that in a given situation the attitude of Christian love must always be that of meek acceptance and the patient smile.

✛

18 July

THE FACT OF FREE WILL

If we knew all the facts, and the effects, both short-term and long-term of human selfishness and evil, a very large proportion of mankind's miseries could be explained. But, of course, this in no way answers the questioner who asks, 'Why doesn't God stop evil and cruel men causing so much suffering?'

This is a very natural and understandable question, but how exactly could such intervention be arranged without interfering with the gift of personal choice? Are we to imagine the possessor of a cruel tongue to be struck dumb, the writer of irresponsible and harmful newspaper articles visited with writer's cramp, or the cruel and vindictive husband to find himself completely paralysed?

Even if we limit God's intervention to the reinforcement of the voice of conscience, what can be done where conscience is disregarded or has been silenced through persistent suppression?

The moment we begin to envisage such interventions, the whole structure of human free will is destroyed.

✤

19 July

'IN THE WORLD... BUT...'

I do not know who started the idea that if men serve God and live their lives to please him, then he will protect them by special intervention from pain, suffering, misfortune and the persecution of evil men. We need look no further than the recorded life of Jesus Christ himself to see that even the most perfect human life does not secure such divine protection.

A great deal of misunderstanding and mental suffering could be avoided if this erroneous idea were exposed and abandoned. How many people who fall sick say, either openly or to themselves, 'Why should this happen to me? I've always lived a decent life.' There are even people who feel that God has somehow broken his side of the bargain in allowing illness or misfortune to come upon them.

But what is the bargain?

If we regard the New Testament as our authority, we shall find no such arrangement being offered to those who open their lives to the living Spirit of God. They are indeed guaranteed that nothing, not even the bitterest persecution, the worst misfortune or the death of the body, can do them any permanent harm or separate them from the love of God. They are promised that no circumstance of earthly life can defeat them in spirit and that the resources of God are always available for them.

Further, they have the assurance that the ultimate purposes of God can never be defeated.

The idea that if a man pleases God, then God will especially shield him belongs to the dim twilight of religion and not to Christianity at all.

'In the world you shall have tribulation, but be of good cheer...' (John 16:33).

✣

20 July

A MAGNIFIED MAN?

The blackness of what we call 'natural disaster' is made far darker than it really is because of modern man's obsession with physical death as the worst evil. Moreover, he will persist in viewing disaster through human eyes.

It is only from the human point of view that the headline, '200 KILLED BY EARTHQUAKE—5,000 HOMELESS' is more distressing than, 'FARMER KILLED BY LIGHTNING, WIDOW PROSTRATED BY GRIEF'. The question, 'How could a God of love allow so many to be killed and so many to suffer?' has really very little sense in it.

We may need the impact of a large-scale piece of human suffering before we are properly impressed, but in the eyes of the sort of God whom Christians worship, the question of number and size is neither impressive nor significant.

To imagine that God looks on physical death as many men do, or to think of him as impressed by numbers, violence or size, is simply to think of God as a magnified man—a monstrously inadequate conception.

21 July

GOOD FROM EVIL

The result of the occurrence of disease and suffering is by no means necessarily evil. It is not in the sentimental novel only that the self-centred husband has been shocked back into responsibility and even into a renewal of true love by the sickness of his wife.

Similarly the illness of a child can and does renew and deepen the love between a husband and wife.

I can recall quite a number of occasions when visiting in hospital men who had never previously been ill in their lives, being told that such a forcible withdrawal from life came to be regarded far more as a friend than as an enemy. 'It gives you a chance to think.' 'It's made me think about God...'

I am sure that disease is in itself evil, but I am left wondering how the courage, love and compassion it evokes would be produced in a world where everybody was perfectly healthy.

✣

22 July

THE ANSWER

I do not believe that we take the question of 'evil' seriously enough in modern days, so that we are continually being disappointed, shocked or horrified by its manifestations.

Although I am very far from subscribing to the doctrines of the total depravity of man, it does seem to me to have been proved within my own lifetime that the problem of human evil is not much affected by better education, better housing, higher wages, holidays with pay, and the National Health Service—desirable as all these things may be for other good reasons.

We need a much more realistic approach to the problem of human evil.

I am perfectly certain that no really effective way of dealing with evil will be found apart from the rediscovery of true religion.

❖

23 July

THE SOURCE OF POWER

The only quality which has patience and strength enough to redeem either people or situations is the quality of outgoing love, the very thing of which we are so lamentably short. If we look at God-become-man, we find that, as a matter of course and of habit, he opened his personality to God, not merely to be sure that he was following the divine plan of action *but to receive potent spiritual reinforcement for the overcoming of evil*.

If this was necessary for him it is so much more necessary for us. Yet how few, even alas among professing Christians, deliberately and of set purpose draw upon the unseen spiritual resources of God?

We are so infected by the prevailing atmosphere of thought, which assumes that nothing can enter our earthly lives from outside, that a great deal of what the New Testament takes for granted does not strike us as realistic or practical.

There are discoveries to be made here which would prove far more revolutionary in the solving of human problems than any purely physical marvels.

24 July

A NEW SCALE OF VALUES

We may think Jesus' free use in the parables of the ideas of rewards, compensations and punishments in 'the life to come' somewhat crude. We like to think that we do good for the sake of doing good and not for any reward or through fear of any punishment. But if we take Christ seriously, we cannot avoid the conclusion that our status in the next stage of existence will be largely determined by our behaviour in this one.

As far as I know, Christ nowhere suggests that we should be 'good', unselfish and loving merely because we shall thereby win a heavenly reward. Nor does he suggest that we should avoid evil merely because we shall otherwise suffer for it hereafter. He is simply concerned to state what he clearly sees to be inevitable consequence. He is neither threatening nor promising, but stating inescapable fact.

His chief call therefore is to what is usually rather misleadingly translated 'repentance', but is actually *metanoia*. That implies *a fundamental change of outlook, the acceptance of a quite different scale of values*.

The call to follow him, to enlist in the service of his Kingdom, must sooner or later include this revolution in thinking.

✛

25 July

REAL SECURITY

I see some clue to the spiritual satisfaction afforded by acceptance of the Christian faith in what have now become established as the psychological essentials of human living. For the distilled wisdom of psychological schools of thought really amounts to this: that human beings need above all *love, security and significance*.

The personality deprived of any of these three, especially during the formative years, is inevitably bound to show signs of inner deprivation.

To put it in plain terms, everybody needs to love and be loved, everybody needs a reasonable degree of security, and everybody needs to feel he holds a significant place in human society. A great many human evils are directly attributable to the fact that people have been or are deprived of these basic requirements.

The conscientious humanist society will do its utmost to meet these psychological needs, but I believe that they must also be recognized at a much deeper level, at the level of the naked and lonely human spirit. Because many people live most of their lives in the company of others, and indeed many cannot bear to be alone, these deep needs are often concealed. But when circumstances force men, possibly through tragedy, bereavement or personal suffering, to realize their solitariness, a need far deeper than the basic psychological requirements is, often poignantly, experienced.

Man finds that he needs both to love and be loved by God. He desperately needs *real* security. He wants the deep security of knowing that he is in fact a son of God, and that there is nothing whatever which could possibly happen to him which can affect the ultimate safety of that relationship.

Spiritually, too, he deeply needs to know that he is of value, that his little gift is significant in the vast eternal scheme of things.

Properly understood, the Christian faith answers all these needs at the deepest level.

✛

26 July

TRUTH AND LOVE

There is apparently a possibility of a man's putting himself outside forgiveness by the 'sin against the Holy Spirit'. This, from an examination of the context, would appear to be a combination of refusing to recognize truth and refusing to allow the heart to love others.

If God himself is both truth and love, it would be logical to suppose that a deliberate refusal to recognize or harbour truth and love would result in an attitude that makes reconciliation with God impossible.

Now if it is true that God is both truth and love, it will readily be seen that the greatest sins will be unreality, hypocrisy, deceit, lying, or whatever else we choose to call sins against truth, and self-love, which makes fellowship with other people and their proper treatment impossible.

Forgiveness must then consist in a restoration to reality, that is, truth and love.

✛

27 July

FORGIVEN

If the Christian religion merely said, 'You must try harder', it would be cold comfort. It doesn't. It says that the faults and failings which we see in ourselves are only outward symptoms of trouble which lies deeper.

We are out of touch with God.

For example, it is no good forgetting the past unless we can be sure it is forgiven as well. Some people have wonderful powers of 'forgetting', or so it appears, but until they are *forgiven*, their lives will never be of greater quality.

Other people, more sensitive perhaps, cannot forget the past. In times of depression, it seems like a great weight round their necks. They can never have anything but a temporary improvement in the sort of lives they lead, until they know that the past is both forgotten and forgiven.

Who can possibly work such a miracle except the living God?

'If we confess our sins,' the New Testament says, 'he is faithful and just to forgive us our sins and to cleanse us from all unrighteousness' (1 John 1:9).

These are old words, but they are true in the experience of thousands. Believe them!

✛

28 July

TO FORGIVE MEANS TO LOVE

Christ unequivocally claimed the right 'to forgive sins', but the grounds on which the sins of men can be forgiven are not, in the recorded words of Christ, the conventional ones presupposed by many Christians.

We find in Christ an intimate connection between forgiveness of sins and the existence of love in a man's heart. 'Forgive us our trespasses as we forgive them that trespass against us' is so familiar in our ears that we hardly grasp the fact that Christ joined fellowship with God and fellowship with other human beings indissolubly.

'Except you from your hearts forgive everyone his trespasses,' he is reported to have said after a particularly telling parable, 'neither will my heavenly Father forgive you your trespasses' (Mark 11:25–26).

Moreover, on one occasion he said of a woman who was apparently something of a notoriety that 'her sins, which are many, are forgiven: for she loved much' (Luke 7:47).

It seems to me consonant with Christ's teaching to hold that love is a prerequisite of forgiveness.

❖

29 July

WHAT A FOOL...

Two young men of the same age choose divergent paths. A is determined to squeeze all the pleasure and enjoyment out of life that he can. B is equally determined to 'get on'. Despite the gibes of his friend, he attends evening classes and works hard in his spare time at his chosen subject.

Suppose that the friends go separate ways and do not meet for several years. When they do B has unquestionably 'got on' and has a responsible, well-paid position. A has advanced very little. His reactions at seeing B again may quite possibly be just unreasonable envy, but equally possibly A may say to himself, 'What a fool I've been! What opportunities I threw away. B is just the sort of man I could have been!'

This naïve little tale illustrates how a genuine 'conviction of sin' may arise. A man who has lived selfishly and carelessly meets someone who has plainly found happiness and satisfaction in co-operating with what he can see of God's purpose. The former may pass the whole thing off as a joke. 'Of course, old so-and-so always was a bit religious'—but he may quite possibly see in the other man the sort of person he himself might have been.

The standard he mocked and the God he kept at arm's length have produced in the other man something he very badly wants.

If his reflection on that situation is, 'What a fool I've been', he, too, is beginning to get a genuine sense of sin.

✢

30 July

SIN...

Suppose that a man who is rather proud of his ability to knock off a quick effective little painting discovers a bit of canvas fastened to a wall. For his own pleasure and the appreciation of his friends he rapidly paints in a bright, effective, and amusing little picture. Stepping back to see his own handiwork better, he suddenly discovers that he has painted his little bit of nonsense on the corner of a vast painting of superb quality, so huge that he had not realized its extent or even that there was a picture there at all.

His feelings are rather like those a man feels when he suddenly sees the vast sweep of God's design in life, and observes the cheap and discordant little effort his own living so far represents when seen against that background.

✢

31 July

THE ENEMY

Christ definitely spoke of a power of spiritual evil. Using the language of his contemporaries, he called this power 'Satan', 'the Devil', or 'the Evil One'.

Whatever mystery lies behind the existence of such an evil spiritual power—whether we accept a Miltonic idea of a fallen angelic power or whether we conceive the evil spirit in the world as arising out of the cumulative effects of centuries of selfish living—there can be no blinking the fact that Christ spoke, and acted, on the assumption that there is a power of evil operating in the world.

If we accept as fact his claim to be God, this must make us think seriously.

We are so accustomed by modern thought to regard evil as 'error', as the 'growing pains' of civilization, or simply as an inexplicable problem, that once more the mind does not readily accept what is in effect God's own explanation—that there is a spirit of evil operating in the world.

We find Christ speaking quite plainly of this spirit as responsible for disease and insanity as well as being the unremitting enemy of those who want to follow the new, true order.

We feel sure that you, whom we love, are capable of better things and will enjoy the full experience of salvation. God is not unfair: he will not lose sight of all that you have done, nor of the loving labour which you have shown for his sake in looking after fellow-Christians (as you are still doing). It is our earnest wish that every one of you should show a similar keenness in fully grasping the hope that is within you, until the end.

HEBREWS 6:9–11

172

August

Now Christ is the visible expression of the invisible God. He was born before creation began, for it was through him that everything was made, whether heavenly or earthly, seen or unseen. Through him, and for him, also, were created power and dominion, ownership and authority. In fact, all things were created through, and for, him. He is both the first principle and the upholding principle of the whole scheme of creation.

COLOSSIANS 1:15–17

1 August

THREE CHEERS!

Once, at a rather difficult youth meeting, I tried to explain what worship meant.

I finally said to the young people, with, I fear, a little exasperation, 'Well, it's three cheers for God!'

In a way, that is not too bad a way of putting it!

2 August

THIS IS YOUR GOD

What sort of person is God?

Christ's answer is quite unequivocal.

He is 'the Father'.

When we hear this familiar truth, we nearly always read back into God's character what we know of fatherhood. This is understandable enough, but it reverses the actual truth. If God is 'the Father', in nature and character and operation, then we derive (if we are parents) our characteristics from him. We are reproducing, no doubt on a microscopic scale and in a thoroughly faulty manner, something of the character of God.

Once we accept it as true that the whole power behind this astonishing universe is of that kind of character that Christ could only describe as 'Father', the whole of life is transfigured.

If we are really seeing in human relationships, fragmentary and faulty yet nevertheless real reflections of the nature of God, a flood of light is immediately released upon all the life that we can see.

People, and our relationships with them, at once become of tremendous importance.

※

3 August

OUR FATHER

When Christ taught his disciples to regard God as their 'Father in heaven', he did not mean that their idea of God must necessarily be based upon their idea of their own fathers. For all we know there may have been many of his hearers whose fathers were unjust, tyrannical, stupid, conceited, feckless, or indulgent.

It is the *relationship* that Christ is stressing.

The intimate love for, and interest in, his son possessed by a good earthly father represents to men a relationship that they can understand, even if they themselves are fatherless!

The same sort of relationship, Christ is saying, can be reliably reckoned upon by man in his dealings with God.

✤

4 August

THE PARENTAL HANGOVER

Because Christ said that men must become 'as little children' (that is, repudiate all the sham, compromise, and cynicism, of adulthood) before they could play their part in the Kingdom with simplicity and sincerity, some have supposed that he places a premium upon human immaturity.

It is ludicrous to suppose that any sensible God can wish adult men and women to crawl about in spiritual rompers in order to preserve a rather sentimental Father–child relationship. Indeed, experience shows that it is only the mature Christian man who can begin to see a little of the 'size' of his Father. He may previously have thought that the comparison of the relationship between the toddler and his grown-up father with his own relationship towards God was rather an exaggeration of the gulf, in intelligence at least. But in his growing maturity he is likely to see that Christ, in his kindness of heart, has certainly not exaggerated the awe-inspiring disparity between man and God.

To have a God, then, who is as much, or more, our superior than we are the superior of an infant child crawling on the hearth-rug, is not to hold a childish concept of God, but rather the reverse. It is only when we limit the mind's stirrings after its Maker by imposing upon it half-forgotten images of our own earthly parents, that we grow frustrated in spirit and wonder why for us the springs of worship and love do not flow.

We must leave behind 'parental hangover' if we are to find a 'big enough' God.

✤

5 August

BIG AND SMALL

To hold a conception of God as a mere magnified human being is to run the risk of thinking of him as simply the Commander-in-Chief who cannot possibly spare the time to attend to the details of his subordinates' lives. Yet to have a god who is so far beyond personality and so far removed from the human context in which we alone can appreciate 'values', is to have a god who is a mere bunch of perfect qualities—which means an idea and nothing more.

We need a God with the capacity to hold, so to speak, both big and small in his mind at the same time.

This, the Christian religion holds, is the true and satisfying conception of God revealed by Jesus Christ.

✤

6 August

THE GOD OF TODAY

Although I am far from subscribing to the Jesuitical doctrine that the end justifies the means, I think we should be prepared to go to almost any length to reveal the living God at work today.

We must not suppose that God has a 'Radio 3' mind or that he shares our veneration for tradition. We may enjoy reading *The Times*, but we must not forget that most pointed and indeed most poignant questions are raised in the correspondence columns of *The Daily Mirror* and *The Sun*.

If the incarnation is as we said earlier, a 'tremendous dive', it is not really such tremendous condescension for you and me to come down to where people are thinking and arguing and yearning and hoping, and help to bring them, not so much 'the God of Abraham and Isaac and Jacob,' about whom most of them couldn't care less, but the God who cares intensely about the men and women of this jet-propelled age.

✜

7 August

'RADIO 3' GOD

All 'lofty' concepts of the greatness of God need to be carefully watched lest they turn out to be mere magnifications of certain human characteristics.

We may, for instance, admire the ascetic ultra-spiritual type which appear to have 'a mind above' food, sexual attraction, and material comfort, for example. But if, in forming a picture of the holiness of God, we are simply enlarging this spirituality and asceticism to the 'nth' degree, we are forced to some peculiar conclusions. Thus we may find ourselves readily able to imagine God's interest in babies (for are they not 'little bits of heaven'?), yet be unable to imagine his approval, let alone design, of the acts which led to their conception!

Similarly it is natural and right, of course, that the worship we offer to God in public should be of the highest possible quality. But that must not lead us to conceive a musically 'Radio 3' god who prefers the exquisite rendering of a cynical, professional choir to the ragged bawling of sincere but untutored hearts.

✜

8 August

SECONDHAND GOD

Conclusions as to the nature of life and God can only in very rare instances be inferred from the artificial evidence of fiction. We need therefore to be constantly on our guard against the 'secondhand God'—the kind of god which the continual absorption of fictional ideas nourishes at the back of our minds. One tiny slice of real life, observed at first hand, provides better grounds for our conclusions than the whole fairy world of fiction.

The author of fiction (and this is not the least of the attractions of authorship) is in the position of a god to his own creatures. He can move in a mysterious way, or an outrageous way, or an unjust way, his wonders to perform; and no one can say him nay.

If he works skilfully (as, for instance, did Thomas Hardy) he may strongly infect his reader with, for example, the sense of a bitterly jesting fate in place of God. He can communicate heartbreak by the simplest of manipulations, because he is himself providence, but he is not thereby providing any evidence of the workings of real life.

The whole tragedy of King Lear might be said to depend on Shakespeare's manipulation of the character of Cordelia. Because she is unable to see (though every schoolgirl in the pit can see) the probable consequence of her blunt 'Nothing', the tragedy is launched.

But it would be a profound mistake to confuse the organized disasters of even the greatest writer of tragedy with the complex circumstances and factors which attend the sufferings of real life.

✣

9 August

GOD IN A HURRY

If there is one thing which should be quite plain to those who accept the revelation of God in nature, and the Bible, it is that he is *never* in a hurry. Long preparation, careful planning, and slow growth, would seem to be leading characteristics of spiritual life.

Yet there are many people whose religious tempo is feverish. With a fine disregard for its context they flourish like a banner the text, 'The King's business requireth haste' (1 Samuel 21:8), and proceed to drive themselves and their followers nearly mad with tension and anxiety!

It is refreshing, and salutary, to study the poise and quietness of Christ.

His task and responsibility might well have driven a man out of his mind.

But he was never in a hurry, never impressed by numbers, never a slave of the clock.

He was acting, he said, as he observed God to act. He was never in a hurry.

✢

10 August

ONE HUNDRED PER CENT GOD

Of all the false gods, there is probably no greater nuisance in the spiritual world than the 'God of one hundred per cent'. For he is plausible.

It can so easily be argued that since God is perfection, and, since he asks the complete loyalty of his creatures, the best way of serving, pleasing, and worshipping him is to set up absolute one-hundred-per-cent standards and see to it that we obey them. After all, did not Christ say, 'Be ye perfect'? (Matthew 5:48).

This one-hundred-per-cent standard is a real menace to Christians of various schools of thought, and has led quite a number of sensitive conscientious people to what is popularly called a nervous breakdown.

It has also taken the joy and spontaneity out of the Christian lives of many more who dimly realize that what was meant to be a life of 'perfect freedom' has become only an anxious slavery.

÷

11 *August*

A DISAPPOINTMENT?

The people who feel that God is a disappointment have not understood the terms on which we inhabit this planet. They want a world in which good is rewarded and evil is punished—as in a well-run kindergarten. They want to see the good man prosper invariably, and the evil man suffer invariably, here and now.

There is, of course, nothing wrong with their sense of justice. But they misunderstand the conditions of this present temporary life in which God withholds his hand, in order, so to speak, to allow room for his plan of free will to work itself out.

Justice will be fully vindicated when the curtain falls on the present stage, when the house-lights go on, and we go out into the Real World.

There will always be times when, from our present limited point of view, we cannot see the wood for the trees. Glaring injustice and pointless tragedy will sometimes be quite beyond our control and our understanding.

We can, of course, postulate an imaginary God with less good sense, love and justice than we have ourselves. And we may find a perverse pleasure in putting blame on him.

But that road leads nowhere.

You cannot worship a disappointment.

÷

12 *August*

GOD FOR THE ÉLITE

Some modern Christians regard mystics as being somehow a cut above their fellows, a sort of spiritual élite. Ordinary forms of worship and prayer may suffice for the ordinary man, but the one who has direct apprehension of God—he is literally in a class by himself.

You cannot expect a man to attend Evensong in his parish church when there are visions waiting for him in his study!

The New Testament does not subscribe to this flattering view of those with a gift for mystic vision. It is always downright and practical.

It is by their fruits that men shall be known. God is no respecter of persons. True religion is expressed by such humdrum things as visiting those in trouble and steadfastly maintaining faith despite exterior circumstances.

It is not, of course, that the New Testament considers it a bad thing for a man to have a vision of God, but there is a wholesome insistence on such a vision being worked out in love and service.

✣

13 August

GOD OF THE LIVING

There are quite a number of religious people who might fairly be said to be more at home with Jehovah than with Jesus Christ. The Old Testament, again if the truth were told, means more to them than the New.

These are the people who see religion as a contract. They obey certain rules and so God will faithfully look after them and their interests.

These are the people who write to the papers and say 'if only' the nation would obey the Ten Commandments, then God would grant victory, or rain, or fine weather, or whatever the need of the moment may be.

They like everything cut-and-dried. Even the Gospel is reduced to a formula, so that if you sign on the dotted line, so to speak, you are all right for heaven! They prefer the letter to the spirit and definite commandments to vague principles. They more usually refer to 'the Lord' than to 'God'.

Such people have not appreciated the revolutionary character of God's invasion of the world in Christ, though they would be horrified if it were suggested that they have not yet accepted the import of his pronouncement: 'Ye have heard that it was said of old time… but I say unto you…'

Their Old Testament God will not suffice for the hunger of modern man, however they may wring their hands at the 'unbelief' of today.

God is not a God of the dead, but of the living.

✛

14 August

AN ADEQUATE GOD

God must not be limited to religious matters or even to the 'religious' interpretation of life.

He must not be confined to one particular section of time nor must we imagine him as the local god of this planet or even only of the universe that astronomical survey has so far discovered.

It is not, of course, physical size that we are trying to establish in our minds. Physical size is not important. By any reasonable scheme of values, a human being is of vastly greater worth than a mountain ten million times his physical size. It is rather to see the immensely broad sweep of the Creator's activity, the astonishing complexity of his mental processes which science laboriously uncovers, the vast sea of what we can only call 'God', for it is in a small corner of this that man 'lives and moves and has his being'.

15 August

TO BE SOMETHING

There is a certain spiritually masochistic joy in being crushed by the juggernaut of a negative god. This is perfectly brought out in a hymn which is still sung in certain circles:

> *Oh to be nothing, nothing*
> *Only to live at His feet*
> *A broken and emptied vessel*
> *For the Master's use made meet.*

The sense of humour is, of course, suspended by the negative god, or his devotees would be bound to see the absurdity of anyone's ambition being to be 'nothing', a 'broken' and, not unnaturally, 'emptied' vessel lying at God's feet! Better still, the New Testament (a book full of freedom and joy, courage and vitality) might be searched in vain to supply any endorsement whatsoever of the above truly dreadful verse and the conception of God it typifies.

If ever a book taught men to be 'something, something', to stand and do battle, to be far more full of joy and daring and life than they ever were without God—that book is the New Testament!

✤

16 August

THE PURPOSE OF LIFE

What is the purpose of life?

Christ did not give an answer to this question in its modern cynical form which implies, 'Is it worth living at all?' but he did answer those who wanted to know what to do with the vitality, affections, and talents, with which they were endowed.

He also answered those who already saw intuitively that this present life was transitory and incomplete and wanted to know how to be incorporated into the main timeless Stream of Life itself.

The questions are really much the same. In both cases men wanted to know how they could be at one with life's real purpose. And of course they still do.

Jesus said that there were really two main principles of living on which all true morality and wisdom might be said to depend. The first was to *love God with the whole personality*, and the second to *love his fellow men as much and in the same way as he naturally loved himself*.

If these two principles were obeyed, Christ said that a man would be in harmony with the Purpose of Life, which transcends time.

These two principles, one of which deals with the invisible and unchanging, the other with the visible and variable, cover the total relationships of a man's life.

Christ made them intensely practical and indissolubly connected.

❖

17 August

TWO MISTAKES

Critics often complain that, if the world is in its present state after nineteen centuries of Christianity, then it cannot be a very good religion.

They make two mistakes.

In the first place Christianity—the real thing—has never been accepted on a large scale and has therefore never been in a position to control 'the state of the world', though its influence has been far from negligible.

In the second place, they misunderstand the nature of Christianity. It is not to be judged by its success or failure to reform the world which rejects it.

If it failed where it is accepted, there might be grounds for complaint, but it does not so fail.

It is a revelation of the true way of living, the way to know God, the way to live life of eternal quality. It is not to be regarded as a handy social instrument for reducing juvenile delinquency or the divorce rate!

✧

18 August

HARMONIOUS LIVING

We cannot love 'to order', but we have the power to choose where we shall bestow our affections and loyalties. We can choose whether we turn them in upon ourselves, whether we give them to false impermanent gods of our own making, or whether we deliberately set them upon the very highest that we know.

Christ knew the secret of happy, effectual and harmonious living, both for individuals and for nations. It is simply this—to love God first with the whole of our powers and personalities, and then to extend to others the deep-seated love we have for ourselves.

But the order of these two principles cannot be reversed: to love God with heart and soul and mind and strength, remains the first and great commandment.

✧

19 August

HUMAN COMMITMENT

Our crosses are not likely to be Christ's Calvary. But nevertheless, no situation or relationship is ever permanently changed, and certainly no human personality is ever radically altered, except at the cost of self-giving love.

It is nonsensical to suppose that we can achieve anything for the kingdom of God by merely sitting secure in our own salvation. We are called to the same costly involvement in the human situation as was Christ himself.

There are religions, fashionable in some quarters, which offer detachment from this passing world and the peace which comes from non-participation in its struggles. But no one could look honestly at the cross and say that this is the way to which we are called.

It is true that our roots, our ultimate security, are in the eternal God. But the teaching, the life and death of Christ show quite plainly that we are called to live lives of close human commitment.

We are to be humanists in the name of the Lord our God!

✣

20 August

ETERNAL LIFE NOW

Let me draw attention to a fact which once firmly grasped by heart and mind affects a man's life both here and in what we call the 'hereafter'.

Consider his words, 'He that heareth my word, and believeth on him that sent me, *hath* everlasting life' (John 5:24). What is this but a plain assurance that if a man accepts the teaching of Christ as the fundamental expression of the Father's authority and plan, he enters already upon that timeless quality of living which is sometimes called 'eternal life'?

In other words, if a man uses his faith-faculty to grasp with heart and mind the essential truth about life, he becomes part of Real Life.

'According to your faith be it unto you' (Matthew 9:29).

These words take on a new meaning if we are thinking of faith, not as a desperate effort to believe, so much as the using of a faculty to grasp unseen realities and utilize unseen resources.

✛

21 August

RADIANT FAITH

A human being can, in a real sense, 'know' God through Christ and Christ himself can be truly alive to him.

I have seen this recognition and knowledge of God in people of all denominations, in men and women of several different nationalities, as well as those who belong to various social strata.

I have known clever scientists as well as men of the highest calibre in literature or the arts who regard God with the deepest awe and at the same time know him through Christ almost as a personal friend.

I have known people of a much simpler cast of mind, who would probably not be able to pass any formal examinations, who have a sturdy and invincible faith in God their Father and similarly find Christ a real person.

It is true that the comparatively unintelligent will sometimes use naïve terms in speaking of God, but I have never found a true Christian without a profound sense of awe and wonder.

I cannot help being impressed by what I have seen and by what people have told me. The laboratory-check for spiritual experience is life itself, and it is exactly here, sometimes in the most appallingly dangerous and painful situations that I have found faith both sure and radiant.

In short, I have seen the experience of God, described in the New Testament, occurring again and again in our modern world.

22 August

NO ARMCHAIR PHILOSOPHER

Paul has his detractors. There are those who feel he is like the man who says 'I don't want to boast, but…', and then proceeds to do that very thing!

Let us look at his list of 'boasting'. We have only to turn up 2 Corinthians 11:23–27.

Have any of us gone through a tenth of that catalogue of suffering and humiliation? Yet this is the man who can not only say that in all these things we are more than conquerors, but can also 'reckon that the sufferings of this present time are not worthy to be compared with the glory which shall be revealed in us' (Romans 8:18).

Here is no armchair philosopher, no ivory-tower scholar, but a man of almost incredible drive and courage, living out in actual human dangers and agonies the implications of his unswerving faith.

✛

23 August

RELIGIONLESS CHRISTIANITY

Phrases such as 'religionless Christianity' are bandied about as though we had outgrown God. But if we read the *Letters and Papers from Prison* by the Christian martyr, Dietrich Bonhoeffer, to whom this phrase is attributed, it is obvious that he did not mean anything of the kind. He was protesting against religion divorced from life—and what true Christians wouldn't? But he was also a deeply religious man to the day of his death.

Yet the phrase sticks.

The modern humanist, with his irrational prejudice against anything 'supernatural', welcomes the idea of a sort of Christianity without religion. But, of course, true Christianity is rooted in both God and man.

The New Testament gives no sort of endorsement to modern man's extraordinary illusion of being able to dispense with God.

24 August

HEIGHT AND DEPTH

There are several modern writers who pour scorn upon any idea of God being *up* and *above*. They are of course confusing literal spatial position with a mental image which must be common to nearly all thinking human beings.

Why should we talk of *high* ideals or a *high* purpose? Why should we talk of a *rise in salary*?

Why should sales be *soaring*?

Why should a boy be promoted from the *Lower* to the *Upper* Fifth form?

Why does an important person in our judiciary sit in a *high* court?

All this simply is a common and understandably symbolic way of speaking. Quite naturally, the converse is equally true. In the same way in ordinary speech a man may *fall* in our estimation, a failing business is fast *going downhill*, some people are of *low* intelligence and some unfortunates have *sunk to the depths*, and so on.

As I studied Paul's letters, I became convinced that he uses expressions of height and depth as useful symbols, but not as geographical locations.

25 August

HIGH PLACES

When Paul writes that 'God raised Christ from the dead and set him at his own right hand in the heavenly places, far above all principality and power, and might, and dominion, and every name that is named, not only in this world, but also in that which is to come', does anyone seriously imagine that Paul, or the Ephesian Christians to whom he was writing, thought of this exaltation as being measurable in physical terms?

Again, in the same letter to Ephesus, when Paul asserts that the Christian's real battle is against spiritual rather than physical enemies and mentions 'spiritual wickedness in high places', does anyone seriously suggest that Paul meant demonic goings-on at the Emperor's court?

Of course not!

To Paul there was a heavenly reality which at present we may sense but not see, and the earthly reality which is discernible by the senses but doomed, like all creation, to ultimate decay.

The 'bright blue sky' stuff belongs to Victorian piety and not the New Testament.

✤

26 August

ANSWERS TO PRAYER

I remember one of my scouts keeping a record in a notebook of the answers to his prayers. He once came to me in great delight and said: 'Do you know, I find it works out at forty-nine to one in favour of God answering my prayers!'

I must confess I was completely stumped for a suitable reply! What we call prayer is deliberately putting ourselves in touch with the One who made us, and who is 'in charge of' the whole universe. Quite apart from our private requests, we need this contact to keep us spiritually clean, to gain strength and inspiration, and last but by no means least, to listen to his orders.

How few of all the millions in the world are even trying to cooperate with the One who designed the whole scheme of things.

We who are longing for a better world should take the time and trouble to get in touch with God and find out the sort of things that he wants done.

✦

27 August

SPIRITUAL EXPERIMENTS

Jesus told men 'to know', 'to seek', and 'to ask', by which I understand him to mean that although the resources of God are always available, it is up to us men to make use of them.

I think too, that he may well have meant men to make spiritual experiments, to try out, as it were, the divine resource. As we do this, we shall inevitably find that the values and fortunes of this passing world become less important and clamant.

Nevertheless, I think we should be wise, by deliberately training ourselves, to see that real security does not, indeed cannot, rest in this world, however lucky or careful we may be.

28 August

BOTH/AND

We seem to live in an atmosphere of 'either/or' whereas it is really a matter of 'both/and'.

It is useless to preach a gospel of the soul's redemption to a starving man. But it is equally valueless (and the world around is full of examples) to make men affluent in this world and at the same time deprive them of any sense of God or any meaningful life after death.

Compassion and charity are both popular words today, while faith in God is regarded as largely irrelevant. But in fact both compassion and charity can be monstrously misused unless they are informed by the love of God. Hence we get situations in which compassion goes out to the violent thug who assaults an old lady for her meagre savings, but none at all to her!

Charity means instant social acceptance for the adulterer but little compassion for his deceived and deprived wife.

To love God is the first and greatest commandment, said Jesus, and this is the priority insisted on throughout the New Testament.

29 August

THE RETURN

A man may travel much faster than sound, but that does not help him in the least to deal with the problem of his own marriage which is fast breaking up.

He may successfully launch an artificial satellite, but that does nothing to solve the squalid conditions in which his fellow men have to live only a few streets away.

He may invent and produce commercially 3-D television for every home, but he has not made the slightest contribution towards solving the problems that arise in home, industry and nation—the selfishness, cruelty and greed, the fears, resentments, and suspicions, that poison our common life.

Perhaps the time is not too distant when the bankruptcy of scientific achievements to solve human problems will become increasingly obvious.

Perhaps man will then return, not indeed to rediscover any old-fashioned 'hell-fire' religion, but to seek realistically that quality of living which transforms personality, and which we may fairly call 'New Testament Christianity'.

30 August

IF...

If the Church is to revive and become once more ablaze with the truth of God and full of the warmth of his love, its members must be prepared to meet the cost and make the sacrifice.

The by-product will be, of course, the maintenance of a high level in the spiritual life of the individual members.

For the real danger to professing Christians lies not in the more glaring and grosser temptations and sins, but in a slow deterioration of vision, a slow death to daring, courage, and the willingness to adventure.

❖

31 August

THE MAJOR PREMISE

It is a great help in facing life to believe that the final answers, the ultimate outcome, can never be settled in this particular phase of our existence.

To the man without faith, this appears to be both a piece of evasion of real issues in that it shelves difficult problems, and a piece of wishful thinking in that it believes in the ultimate goodness of God in some nebulous hereafter, even though the daily evidence of life denies such goodness and love.

It is probably quite impossible to explain the Christian attitude to the thoroughgoing materialist, simply because the major premise which makes the whole position tenable and satisfactory is God, and the materialist denies such a person's existence. But, speaking as one who did not arrive at his present convictions without a good deal of questing and questioning, I would assure the materialist that his position looks every bit as ridiculous and untenable to the man who has some small knowledge of God as the Christian position does to the materialist!

You cannot deny a new dimension once you have experienced it.

❖

As, therefore, God's picked representatives, purified and beloved, put on that nature which is merciful in action, kindly in heart and humble in mind. Accept life, and be most patient and tolerant with one another, always ready to forgive if you have a difference with anyone. Forgive as freely as the Lord has forgiven you. And, above everything else, be truly loving, for love binds all the virtues together in perfection.

COLOSSIANS 3:12–14

September

At the beginning God expressed himself. That personal expression, that word, was with God and was God, and he existed with God from the beginning. All creation took place through him, and none took place without him. In him appeared life and this life was the light of mankind. The light still shines in darkness, and the darkness has never put it out.

JOHN 1:1–5

❖

1 September

MIRACLES

A 'miracle' is, by definition, something to be wondered at. In the past, when laws then unknown were being used, it was commonly assumed that the divine intervention was the cause of the wonder. People thought that God was somehow 'interfering' with the working of Nature.

I do not regard such an action as 'impossible' (who are we to say what is 'possible' and what is 'impossible'?), but I think it is unlikely. The vast and patient labours of all kinds of scientists reveal a consistency of natural order, but at the same time they discover complex laws which mankind never knew before.

A distinguished professor of Physics and Chemistry who is a Fellow of the Royal Society, once said to me, 'We labour for years to unlock one door, only to discover that we are confronted with six more locked ones!'

I have met a few other really distinguished scientists in one field or another and each has said, in effect, 'how little we know'.

It therefore seems to me stupid to say that this or that is 'impossible', however simply or naïvely it may be described.

❖

2 September

MORE MIRACLES

Radio and sound reproduction have been my hobby since my school days. I could 'make' (and that means only connect together the components of) a television set. But to understand the principles that lie behind modern electronic circuitry increases my sense of wonder rather than reduces it.

Men are discovering almost every day some new law of Nature, which has been there all the time. Less than a century ago not only radio, radar and television but even such everyday objects of use as electric light and the telephone would have been completely unknown to the vast majority of people. If men and women of the early 1800s had suddenly been shown a television screen which was showing a picture of an event taking place (via a man-made satellite) three thousand miles away, they would without doubt have called it a miracle (as indeed it is). But the laws which make the feat of skill and ingenuity a visible and audible experience have been there for countless aeons of time.

There are literally thousands of such 'miracles' in various departments of human life today. To me, even where I understand and can apply the principles I retain my sense of wonder.

But I cannot for the life of me understand those who automatically rule out the 'miracles' of the Gospels.

✤

3 September

HISTORIC IRRUPTION

I have heard professing Christians of our own day speak as though the historicity of the Gospels does not matter—all that matters is the contemporary Spirit of Christ.

I contend that the historicity *does* matter.

I do not see why we, who live nearly two thousand years later, should call into question an event for which there were many eye-witnesses still living at the time when most of the New Testament was written.

It was no 'cunningly devised fable' but an historic irruption of God into human history which gave birth to a young Church so sturdy that the pagan world could not stifle or destroy the miracle.

✤

4 September

UNCANNY

I must confess that, for years, I had viewed the Greek of the New Testament with a rather snobbish disdain! I had read the best of classical Greek both at school and Cambridge for over ten years. To come down to the *Koine* of the first century AD seemed, as I have sometimes remarked rather uncharitably, like reading Shakespeare for some years then turning to the vicar's letter in the Parish Magazine!

I think now that I was wrong. I can see that the expression of the Word of God in ordinary workaday language is all of a piece with God's incredible humility in becoming Man in Jesus Christ. The language is not as pedestrian as I had at first supposed. Although I did my utmost to preserve an emotional detachment, I found again and again that the material under my hands was strangely alive. It spoke to my condition in the most uncanny way.

I say 'uncanny' for want of a better word, but it was a very strange experience to sense, not occasionally but almost continually, the living quality of those rather strangely assorted books.

To me it is the more remarkable because, as I have said, I had no fundamentalist upbringing. Although as a priest of the Anglican Church, I had a great respect for the Holy Scripture, this very close contact of several years of translation produced an effect of 'inspiration' which I have never experienced, even in the remotest degree, in any other work.

✤

5 September

'I WAS THERE'

Apart from the Gospel which he was inspired to write, almost certainly in Rome itself, we know little more of John Mark as a man.

It was probably his mother's home which was 'furnished and prepared' for the Last Supper (Mark 14:15). This must mean that Mark's mother knew of the secret rendezvous, and very possibly of the curious clue of the man bearing a pitcher of water who would show them where to go—curious because in those days it would have been most unusual for anyone except a woman to carry water.

I hazard a guess that Mark was quite a young man, perhaps even a student at this time. There is strong tradition that he was a Levite and that meant some years of training.

He was not present at the Last Supper, but it is perfectly possible that he saw Judas' departure and knew its significance. He might easily have known where Jesus and the eleven were going. What could be easier for a young man in the eastern equivalent of a night-shirt to slip out and hide in the olive bushes of the Garden? Otherwise how can we explain that Mark alone records Jesus' contemptuous words when the soldiers arrived to arrest him? (Mark 14:48–49).

And who but he would know that an incautious move on his part would make his nightdress visible in the torchlight so that he had to run home as naked as the day he was born?

It surely is his modest way of saying 'I was there'.

❖

6 September

AUTHENTIC

According to an ancient but reliable tradition, Papias, a bishop in Asia Minor in the second century, wrote that Mark 'wrote down accurately everything that Peter remembered'. This might account for some vivid details such as the groups in their vari-coloured robes lying on the green grass at the feeding of the five thousand looking 'like flower-beds' (Mark 6:40).

It is Mark's Gospel that tells us that Jesus was asleep on 'the rower's cushion' during the storm on the lake (Mark 4:38).

It is he who uses a most extraordinary Greek word when describing Jesus' action when taking little children into his arms. It is a rare and intimate word and almost means 'cuddled'.

Then there is that brief sketch of Jesus striding ahead of his disciples to his inevitable death in Jerusalem, while the disciples follow at a distance, frightened and bewildered.

How absolutely authentic Mark's Gospel feels!

✣

7 September

AN AUTHOR IN A HURRY

There is reason to believe that Mark is writing in a hurry.

In the winter of AD64–65, Rome was set ablaze by the Emperor Nero and he unhesitatingly placed the blame at the door of the Christians. Comparatively few people could read and write, even in Rome, and most of the teaching of Jesus and of the apostles, particularly Paul and Peter, had been carefully memorized and was passed on by word of mouth.

As far as we know Mark was the first evangelist who wrote down what the collect for St Mark's day calls 'the heavenly doctrine' of Jesus, the Son of Man and Son of God. It was important that a written record (possibly cunningly hidden) should survive the possible death of all Christians in Rome.

Mark, like all Jews, spoke Aramaic (a popular form of Hebrew) and certainly Jesus did the same. It is interesting to note how again and again Mark gives us the Aramaic words, such as *talitha cumi*, *ephphatha* and *abba*, and follows them immediately with a translation into the sort of Greek which would be widely known in Rome and by a great number of Jews and Gentiles throughout the Empire.

Mark is trying to reach the widest possible public.

Mark is in no doubt that the subject of his rather hastily told story is the Son of God.

But he stresses too the very real humanity of the man Jesus.

✣

8 September

ST LUKE TODAY

Luke was a man of compassion. The underprivileged, which in those days meant nearly all women and nearly all 'foreigners', are given special prominence in his record of the life of Jesus.

He must have done some research too! But for Luke we should not know that matchless parable of God's forgiveness which we call the story of the prodigal son. And we should not know that story, perhaps the most moving of all the resurrection records, of the walk to Emmaus.

Luke has been an inspiration to countless doctors who share his concern for people.

Most of us grumble at times about our own Health Service, sometimes perhaps with reason.

But we must remember too that army of dedicated men and women who are the St Lukes of our day.

✣

9 September

THE EVERLASTING PURPOSE

There are many everyday activities which you can do without the slightest reference to God or to faith in him. You can eat your meals, play games, go out in the car, study without any thought of faith in God. But the moment you begin to consider seriously what you are going to do with your life, and how you can best spend your talents and energies, you come right up against this question of God and his purpose.

Of course, you don't have to! Millions never give the matter a thought, and get through life as best they can. But is such negative drifting very pleasing in the eyes of God?

If you want the highest, the best, the most useful and the most satisfying, we must seek that part of God's plan which he has for us, whether it be important or unimportant in the eyes of the world, or not.

When this little life is over, nearly all that makes the headlines in the newspapers or fills the bulletins on the radio will seem to be of purely temporary significance.

But the work of those who have co-operated with God will remain, for it is part of his everlasting purpose.

✤

10 September

DOWN WITH THESE WALLS!

The man of science has no right to dismiss a religion such as Christianity as a mere hangover from more primitive days. He surely cannot seriously imagine that men of similar intellectual calibre to his own have not asked the same searching fundamental questions about life and its meaning which he himself asks, and yet have come to the conclusion that the Christian faith is an indispensable part of total truth.

If it is rare to find a bishop, shall we say, giving time and thought to understand the elements of a scientific process, it is, in my experience at least, also rare to find a scientist giving his serious attention to the meaning and significance of Christianity.

Surely there need not be such divisive walls between art, science and religion, erected and maintained only too often by pride, ignorance and prejudice.

No intelligent seeker after truth imagines that he is the only one on the right track.

❖

11 September

FOR OUR DECISION

A life lived for a mere thirty years in a poor occupied territory, itself of small account within the huge Roman Empire, would seem at first sight to be so narrow in outlook and so hedged in by circumstance as to provide very little that is valuable for our modern perplexities.

Traditional piety and reverence have often made men reluctant to admit the paucity of information. In the recorded life of Jesus (as we have seen), not a word has been preserved, for example, about his years of adolescence and early manhood. Yet these are times of painful and difficult adjustment for many human beings, and it might well be thought that a divine example would have been a help to many.

Again, since Jesus was unmarried and was executed while still a young man, we are provided with no divine exemplar for the good marriage, for the successful coping with the problems of middle age, or for the gracious acceptance of the closing phases of earthly life.

But perhaps we are looking for the wrong things. Perhaps what we should look for is not so much a perfect pattern of living for every human age-group, but a revelation of truth which will illuminate the heart and centre of human life and give it a new significance and purpose.

Perhaps the information which we so earnestly seek will be both timeless and of universal application.

Perhaps we shall to some extent be taken into the Creator's confidence, and yet handed back a great deal more responsibility for decision than we bargained for!

12 September

REALITY REVEALED

It is imperative for us moderns to get back to essential Christianity so that we may realize afresh the revolutionary character of its message. We have forgotten its devastating disregard, or even reversal, of current worldly values, and have allowed what we call 'Western civilization', or 'the American way of life' to become more or less God-fearing substitutes for the real thing.

When God made his strange invasion of the life of this planet, the little section of humanity into which he came was obsessed as much as we are today with the importance of such things as power, privilege, success and wealth. By revealing reality, by declaring the Kingdom of God, God-become-man undermined or exposed these false values. He taught (and his teaching is as difficult to follow now as it was then) that what is apparently happening may bear little or no relation to what is really happening.

The reality, according to Jesus, is the establishment and growth of a Kingdom of inner loyalty which transcends all human barriers. Therefore, the realization of the existence of this Kingdom, working for its expansion, living according to its principles, and, if necessary, dying for it, is the real significance of man's temporary existence upon the earth.

✥

13 September

INNER CONFLICTS

If we are quiet before God and allow his Spirit to shine upon our inward state, we shall probably discover more than one conflict which is robbing us of inner peace. The man who lives apart from God may be largely unconscious of his inward conflicts and only aware of their tension.

Of course he may be driven by the sheer force of the tension to a psychiatrist who, if he is a wise one, will help the man to realize the sources of his disharmony. But he still will not be at peace with the nature of things, with his own conscience, and the divine purpose that is being worked out in this world unless the psychiatrist is able to lead him to faith in God.

But, except in unusual cases, the Christian need not turn to the psychiatrist. Either alone with God or with the help of a trusted friend, priest, or minister, he can, if he wishes, see for himself the fierce, hidden resentment, the carefully concealed self-importance, the obstinate and unforgiving spirit, and all the other things which prevent inward relaxation.

✣

14 September

PSYCHIATRY

Psychiatry can, and does, remove certain disabilities and resolve certain conflicts, but it cannot by itself supply our standards or values. It cannot answer any questions outside the immediate range of human personality.

I believe that those who would see in modern psychiatry something at once more efficient and more 'scientific' than true religion are doomed to disappointment. For however excellent psychiatric methods may be, no adjustment can be provided towards any supra-human purpose in life and no connection made with any resource outside human personality.

Such further integration may be, and of course sometimes is, provided, even unconsciously, by the psychiatrist. But that is because he is a man of faith himself, and not because he is a practitioner in psychiatry.

He has to go beyond his function as a scientist if he is to adjust his patient to a world of spiritual reality.

✣

15 September

ON MAN'S SIDE

When a man is first ordained, his heart and mind are rightly filled with 'God's remedy for man's failure'. He is no doubt theologically impeccable but he has very little knowledge of mankind. As he goes on with his work, he grows to love and understand ordinary people. He is often surprised at their ignorance and stupidity, but he is far more often surprised by their good-heartedness, their courage and what I can only describe as their most moving vulnerability.

If his love for men and women is strong and if his mind and heart are kept open, it is not long before his attitude changes. When he was first ordained, he was one hundred per cent on God's side while the men and women to whom he was to minister had little more than a theological existence.

As he grows to know and understand and love *people*, he may easily find himself very much 'on man's side'.

✣

16 September

HOPE

We must distinguish between what is genuine hope and what is called 'wishful thinking'. Hope must always be based upon realities, and in the end upon God, the great Reality. But wishful thinking, though it often sounds like hope, is nothing more than an expression of what we should like to happen.

206

In our ordinary speech, we all of us say such things as, 'I hope so-and-so', when all we really mean is that we *wish* so-and-so would happen. This does not matter very much in common parlance as long as we are quite clear in our own minds that there is a definite distinction between expressing a wish and possessing a hope with real grounds for it.

A very great deal of what passes for hope today is either wishful expectation or the expressed reaction of a mind which is not prepared to face realities. We shall not find in the New Testament a single instance of hope used in any but its genuine sense; that is, *hope rooted in the good purpose of God*.

We have to rid our minds of both pious hopes and wishful thinking before we get down to solid, genuine hope.

✠

17 September

ASSUMPTIONS

In English-speaking countries at least, we breathe such an atmosphere of diffused traditional Christianity that we are apt to take some of the major Christian revelations about God as though they were self-evident—which of course they are not. We assume that kindness is a better thing than intolerance, and love a better thing than hatred. But these elementary assumptions are only true if the Author of the whole bewildering universe is himself kind, understanding, and loving.

Most people, whether inside or outside the churches, attempt at least to believe that 'God is love'. Many non-Christians have not the faintest idea that this is a purely Christian concept, and that before the coming of the Gospel no nation in the world had ever dared to conceive of God as active, personal love.

✤

18 September

THE SECOND COMING

The New Testament is indeed a book full of hope, but we may search in vain for any vague, human optimism.

As a translator of the New Testament I find in it no support whatever for the belief that, one day, all evil will be eradicated from the earth, all problems solved, and health and wealth be every man's portion!

Even among some Christians such a belief is quite commonly held, so that the 'second advent' of Christ is no more and no less than the infinite number of 'comings' of Christ into men's minds.

Of course no one would deny that there are millions of such 'comings' every year, but that is not what the Christian Church believes by the second advent of Christ; and it is most emphatically not what any writer of the New Testament ever meant in foretelling his second coming.

The second coming of Christ, the second irruption of eternity into time, will be immediate, violent and conclusive. The human experiment is to end. Illusion will give way to reality. The temporary will disappear before the permanent. The King will be seen for who he is.

The thief in the night, the lightning flash, the sound of the last trumpet, the voice of God's archangel—all these may be picture-language images, but by no stretch of the imagination do they describe a gradual process.

They are pictures of something sudden, catastrophic and decisive.

❖

19 September

PLAYGROUND OF CRANKS

Unhappily, the whole subject of the second coming has been for many years the playground of cranks and fanatics. This has made us not only shy of dealing with the questions ourselves but reluctant to believe in 'the blessed hope' as a fact at all.

Various people, especially within the last sixty years or so, have manipulated texts of Holy Scripture with little regard to context to prove that Christ would return on this or that day.

I remember a man in 1934 hiring the Queen's Hall in London solemnly to warn the British Empire that Jesus Christ would return in person on, I think, 24 June of that year. So convinced was he of his calculations that he stated at the time that if he were wrong he would 'sink into well-merited obscurity'. He left himself no loophole for later revision of the timetable as others have done. I presume he still lives in his obscurity.

This example is only one of hundreds of misguided people who have thought they could calculate what, on Jesus' own admission, was known only to the Father. But because this important New Testament hope has been the stamping-ground of the fanatical, why should we be cheated altogether of what was essentially a part of early Christian teaching?

❖

20 September

UNPLANNED

Planners as we are, if we envisage the second coming of Christ at all, we see him returning in triumph upon a scene already largely

209

perfected. We think it would be a fine thing if the world were neat and tidy, all problems were solved, all tensions were relaxed, understanding and friendship were worldwide, health and wealth were at their highest peak, when Christ returned, not this time as a helpless babe, but as a King in power and glory.

Of one thing we can be certain—that this high, unfathomable wisdom of God works on quite a different plane from any human planning. The time of the irruption of eternity into time, the moment for God to call the end to the long experiment that we call life, will not be made in consultation with human planners!

Judging from his previous action in human history, God is perfectly capable of choosing an unusual and unlikely moment, as it will appear to human beings. Indeed, if we are to take the words of Jesus seriously, his return to the world or the winding-up of the time and space set-up, whichever way we look at it, is to be in the middle of strife, tension, and fear.

In the letters of the New Testament, it is the same.

The coming of Christ is a blessed hope of intervention, not a personal appearance at a utopian celebration.

✤

21 September

CHRIST WILL COME AGAIN

When have Christians been promised physical security? In the early Church it is evident that they did not even expect it! Their security, their true life was rooted in God, and neither the daily insecurities of the decaying Roman Empire nor the organized persecution which followed later, could affect their basic confidence.

The description which Christ gave of the days that were to come before his return is, in my view, more accurately reproduced in this fear-ridden age than it has ever been before in the course of human history. We do not know the times and seasons, of course, but at least we can refuse to be deceived by the current obsession for physical security in the here-and-now.

While we continue to pray and work for the spread of the Kingdom in this transitory world, we know that its centre of gravity is not here at all. When God decides that the human experiment has gone on long enough, yes, even in the midst of what appears to us confusion and incompleteness, Christ will come again.

This is what the New Testament teaches.

It is for us therefore to be alert, vigilant and industrious, so that his coming will not be a terror but an overwhelming joy.

❖

22 September

'PRAY FOR THOSE WHO...'

If we pray for those who annoy and irritate us and whom we dislike, our dislike is lessened and our understanding is increased.

But we must naturally be perfectly honest about it. We must say to him, who is the Father of us all, in all honesty and simplicity, 'I hate the sight of so-and-so. He (or she) irritates me beyond endurance and always brings out the worst in me. Help me to pray for him (or her).'

It takes considerable courage to embark on this course of action, but the situation is invariably improved, if we do. Sometimes it is revolutionized.

In praying for a person's real self, we grow immeasurably in tolerance and understanding. It is not unknown for instinctive dislike to be transformed into respect, understanding, and even love.

But this will never happen if we insist on maintaining an inner attitude of: 'I can't help it; I always have disliked so-and-so and I always will.'

✣

23 September

HONEST LAUGHTER

Suppose we do not feel thankful. Suppose we are rather cross and resentful?

It is always sensible to be utterly honest with God. It never pays in the spiritual life to pretend. Why should we not start with a reverent grumble? Why should we not 'let off steam' to our heavenly Father?

We can never meet with more perfect understanding.

It can happen that our resentfulness or fearfulness, once they are dissipated, will be melted into the beginnings of feeling thankful. For one of the chief reasons why we do not feel thankful is that *our* plans have gone astray, *our* aims have been thwarted or we feel that *we* have not been properly consulted.

In the presence of our heavenly Father, it is more likely that we can see how childishly we have behaved.

One hoot of honest laughter at our beloved self-importance will do us all the good in the world.

✣

24 September

SELF-GIVING

It is perfectly possible for us to behave kindly, justly, and correctly towards one another, and yet withhold that giving of the 'self' which is the essence of love.

Married people will perhaps more easily appreciate what I am trying to say. A husband may behave with perfect kindness and consideration towards his wife. He may give her a generous allowance. He may do more than his share of the household chores. Indeed, he may do all the things which an ideal husband is supposed to do. But if he withholds 'himself', the marriage will be impoverished.

Women who seem to know these things intuitively would infinitely prefer the husband to be less kind, considerate, and self-sacrificing if only they were sure that he, with all his imperfections and maddening ways, gave 'himself' in love in the marriage.

This principle applies to some extent to all human relationships.

I am pretty certain that it is this costly self-giving love which Paul had in mind in 1 Corinthians 13.

❖

25 September

SELF-LOVE

The second great commandment is that a man should 'love his neighbour as himself'.

These words, I am sure, contain no accidental lapse of speech. We do naturally love ourselves, and no spiritual contortions or inverted pride can ever alter the fact. Surely what Jesus is urging is that that love, that understanding, that 'making allowance', which we normally use for ourselves, should be extended and used to embrace others.

It is true that in other places, Jesus says that a man should 'deny himself'; but this, surely, carries the force of denying his own egotistical temptations. It means self-forgetfulness instead of self-interest. It means voluntary self-giving but not self-contempt.

The business of hating oneself, though it appears virtuous, is in reality one of Satan's most plausible devices.

It keeps a man preoccupied with himself and his sins.

The abject attitude of self-loathing may be natural in the presence of God's holiness, but never do we find in the Bible that God requires its continuance.

Having seen and admitted our faults, the command is to stand, or go, or do.

✤

26 September

THE MASTER PLAN

Peace with God is not a static emotion. It is a positive gift which accompanies our living in harmony with God's plan.

Dante's oft-quoted saying, 'And in His will is our peace', is not to be understood as surrender, resignation, and quiescence. The Christian will discover that he knows God's peace as he is aligned with God's purpose. He may be called upon to be strenuous; but he is inwardly relaxed, because he knows he is doing the will of God.

This sense of knowing that he is co-operating with this purpose defies human analysis, and is always found singularly irritating by the opponent of Christianity. But Christians of all ages, not excepting our own, have found it to be true.

However painful or difficult, or, on the other hand, however inconspicuous or humdrum life may be, the Christian finds his peace in accepting and playing his part in the master plan.

✤

27 September

THE ANGELS' VIEW

We sing a hymn containing these lines:

The Angel armies of the skies
Look down with sad and wondering eyes
To see the approaching Sacrifice.

That is 'only a hymn', but we have at least one piece of evidence from the Gospels that the angels of God are interested in human affairs. For

Jesus himself said, 'I tell you there is joy among the angels in heaven over one sinner that repenteth.'

If there is joy, why should there be not sorrow? And why indeed, should not those other beings which God has created, different though they may be from ourselves, watch the unfolding of the human drama with the deepest interest?

These celestial beings live, as far as we know, perpetually in the Royal Presence. Apart from the fact that they are sometimes used as messengers, seen or unseen, from that world to this, we know nothing of the reasons for their existence.

Nevertheless, it helps sometimes to break, in imagination, the fetters of earth and try to see things from the angels' point of view.

❖

28 September

THE HEAVENLY VISION

It was Paul's sense of mission, Paul's certainty of divine support, and above all Paul's vision that sent the Church into the whole known world.

All through the history of the Church, men have had 'visions'. Where they have been obedient to them, God has done great things. But, alas, there have been many times when men were too bound by tradition or too cowardly to 'obey the heavenly vision'.

If we are disobedient to the 'heavenly vision', we *lose* spiritually. It seems to be a spiritual law that if we do not go forwards, we go backwards. If we harden our hearts or shut our eyes or pretend that God has not spoken to us, we lose something. Not only is God's purpose held up, but we lose the sense of God's presence and power with us.

Many Christians have lost their 'first love' and their heavenly vision and feel miserable because somewhere they have failed to obey a call of God.

29 September

WORKS FOLLOWING

The New Testament, itself a reflection of the life of the early Church, conveys the sense of Christian certainty. There is little or no argument in it, certainly no apology and very little in the way of apologetic.

Men and women had seen the living Son of God. Many of them had seen him die and seen him triumph over death. All of them knew the certainty of his presence with them. They might appear drunk with new wine, but they were in fact intoxicated with such a certainty about God as the world had never yet known!

This certainty which often appeared to the enemies of Christianity as mere cocksureness, or even arrogance, was the direct result of God's personal coming in Christ to our world. To the early Christians, the Christian faith was not a performance, but the invasion of their own little lives by a completely new quality of life. It was nothing less than the life of God himself.

They believed and they knew.

And the Lord confirmed their certainty with 'works following'.

30 September

ENDURE IT

The New Testament is extraordinarily realistic about human troubles. Nowhere there do you find anything approaching the idea that if we lead good lives, we shall be free from trouble. On the contrary, we are told as Christians to expect 'trials', 'temptations' and 'afflictions'.

Paul wrote to Timothy, 'Endure hardness like a good soldier of Jesus Christ' (2 Timothy 2:3). This is a call away from flabby and self-indulgent living to a tougher attitude towards the blows that life can aim at us.

Sometimes there is a call to sheer patient endurance, and this comes frequently in the Epistle of the Hebrews. The author of that letter knows very well that no real Christian puts on any kind of spiritual muscle without faithful endurance.

James actually suggests that we should *welcome* the trials that attack our faith (James 1:2). He wrote that for a very simple reason, namely that the cheerful acceptance of trouble and the patient endurance of it produces an end-product—solid character. So trial and testing is really worth it!

Endure it!

❖

Be careful that nobody spoils your faith through intellectualism or high-sounding nonsense. Such stuff is at best founded on men's ideas of the nature of the world and disregards Christ! Yet it is in him that God gives a full and complete expression of himself in bodily form. Moreover, your own completeness is realized in him, who is the ruler over all authorities, and the supreme head over all powers.

COLOSSIANS 2:8–10

October

Live together in harmony, live together in love, as though you had only one mind and one spirit between you. Never act from motives of rivalry or personal vanity, but in humility think more of each other than you do of yourself. None of you should think only of his own affairs, but consider other people's interests also.

PHILIPPIANS 2:2–3

✤

1 October

THE SPIRITUAL HARVEST

There will be people at Harvest Festival services who are certainly never to be found worshipping God at any other time in church!

I often wonder why this is. Is it the colour and natural pageantry of the corn and tomatoes and grapes and marrows which decorate the church which appeals so strongly? Or is it something much older, something 'in the blood', so to speak, which makes human beings feel that at least at harvest-time some acknowledgment is due to the Creator, without whose laws all our labour would be in vain?

In spite of the popularity of the Harvest Festival, it remains a mystery that its obvious lesson as a parable seems to pass quite unnoticed. The laws of the spiritual harvest are just as inevitable and unalterable as those of the garden, the allotment or the open field. The Bible is not threatening, but simply states a plain fact when it says 'whatsoever a man sows that shall he also reap' (Galatians 6:7). Yet the man who will take great care over his garden or allotment will more often than not take no care at all about his own soul. He vaguely 'hopes for the best'.

What sort of garden, or what sort of allotment would he have if he used the same attitude of mind there?

I suppose it is because the laws of God in the spiritual realm work so quietly and inconspicuously that men either do not notice them or think they can neglect them with complete impunity.

Yet in the long run it is neither physical laws nor scientific laws that will matter, but *spiritual* laws.

❖

2 October

HARVEST-MICE

Every year in the harvest fields of England there are thousands of little tragedies. The victims are those charming little creatures, the harvest-mice.

Earlier in the year, the growing corn seems to them to be the ideal place in which to settle and bring up a family. Food, shelter and building material are there in plenty, and everything seems perfectly adapted for their needs. The forest of innumerable corn-stalks is their whole world, and in it they court and play, mate and bring up their families. Their happiness seems to be complete.

Until the harvest. For when the day comes for the owner of the field to reap his harvest, tragedy inevitably begins for the harvest-mouse. The whole world of waving corn which seemed so snug and secure, so specially designed for his comfort and nourishment, comes crashing about his ears.

The field which he thought was his world never really belonged to him at all, and the fact that the growing corn was not meant for his food and shelter has, alas, not entered his tiny head.

❖

3 October

TOWARDS THE HARVEST

The life of the harvest-mouse is not a bad picture of the way in which some people live in the world. They too work and play, court and get married and bring up their children in the happy belief that it is their world, and that to believe in an eventual 'harvest' is old-fashioned and silly. Yet Jesus Christ, who claimed to be the Son of God, said quite plainly that this world is like a field that belongs to God and that it is moving inevitably towards a harvest.

You can read his words about it in St Matthew's Gospel, chapter 13, verses 24–43.

For this little world is not, as some imagine, a permanent thing at all.

When God decides that his great experiment has gone on long enough, he will reap his harvest.

'The harvest is the end of the world,' said Jesus (Matthew 13:39).

❖

4 October

MICE OR MEN?

The field-mouse is deceived because for months he is left to his own devices. He never sees the owner of the field and naturally knows nothing of the coming harvest.

Many people allow themselves to be deceived because God, the Owner of the world, does not put in an appearance, and for the purposes of the experiment we call life, does not interfere with man's power to choose. Many of them imagine that the 'field' belongs to man and that there is no such thing as an eventual 'harvest'.

But if Christ really was, as he claimed to be, God, then his statement about this world being an experimental field with an inevitable harvest should surely be most seriously considered.

No one could blame the little harvest-mouse for not realizing the true purpose of the corn-field or the certainty of the eventual reaping.

But what are we—mice or men?

⁜

5 October

GOD'S WORLD

This is God's world. Although he lays no finger on our free will; although it may take a long time to discover it, that world can only work satisfactorily in harmony with his will.

The harvest is a simple reminder of the mystery that lies behind all that we call life. It is a parable in earthly terms of spiritual realities. It is a profound mistake to think of the laws of God as applying to our allotment or garden, and then fail to see that they also operate in the lives of men and of nations.

'The earth is the Lord's and the fullness thereof.' There is no happiness for the individual and no chance of security except by the full recognition by both heart and mind of that essential fact.

The devil's illusion, from the Garden of Eden onwards, is that the earth is man's.

The fact is, as the psalmist said long ago: 'The earth is the Lord's and the fullness thereof' (Psalm 24:1).

✣

6 October

ROBES AND RITUAL

The Greek word for 'thanksgiving' in the New Testament is a beautiful one, although it looks a bit odd when transliterated into English. It is *eucharistia*.

Poor word! It has become associated in some people's minds with 'High Church', with robes, with bells and smells and ritual! But is has never meant that. It means simply the act of giving thanks to God, of recognizing his greatness and our smallness, his wisdom and our ignorance.

The Church used this word in its earliest years so before long it became attached to the Lord's Supper, the Holy Communion. For here, above everywhere else, we express our thankfulness to a God who gave himself, and gives himself, to us.

Our rather feeble return, though it is the best we can do, is to give *ourselves* to him without reserve.

✣

7 October

MEEK AND MILD

It is a thousand pities that the word 'child' has so few words that rhyme with it appropriate for a hymn. But for this paucity of language we might have been spared the couplet that hundreds of thousands must have learned in their childhood:

> *Gentle Jesus, meek and mild*
> *Look upon a little child.*

But perhaps it was not the stringencies of verse-making that led the writer to apply the word 'mild' to Jesus Christ, for here it is in another children's hymn and this time at the beginning of the line:

> *Christian children all must be*
> *Mild, obedient, good as He.*

Why 'mild'?

✣

8 October

MILD! NEVER!

Of all the epithets that could be applied to Christ 'mild' seems one of the least appropriate. For what does 'mild', as applied to a person, conjure up in our minds? Surely a picture of someone who wouldn't say the proverbial 'boo' to the proverbial goose; someone who would let sleeping dogs lie and avoid trouble wherever possible; someone of a placid temperament who is almost a stranger to the passions of red-blooded humanity; someone who is a bit of a nonentity, both uninspired and uninspiring.

The word 'mild' is apparently deliberately used to describe a man who did not hesitate to challenge and expose the hypocrisies of the religious people of his day; a man who had such 'personality' that he walked unscathed through a murderous crowd; a man so far from being a nonentity that he was regarded by the authorities as a public danger; a man who could be moved to violent anger by shameless exploitation or by smug complacent orthodoxy; a man of such courage that he deliberately walked to what he knew would mean death, despite the earnest pleas of well-meaning friends!

Mild!

What a word to use for a personality whose challenge and strange attractiveness nineteen centuries have by no means exhausted!

Jesus Christ might well be called 'meek', in the sense of being selfless and humble and utterly devoted to what he considered right, whatever the personal cost; but 'mild', never!

✛

9 October

NO SAINT!

We hear, or read, of someone who was a 'real saint'. He 'never saw any harm in anyone and never spoke a word against anyone all his life'. If this really is Christian saintliness, then Jesus Christ was no saint.

It is true that he taught men not to sit in judgment upon one another, but he never suggested that they should turn a blind eye to evil or pretend that other people were faultless.

He himself indulged no roseate visions of human nature. He 'knew what was in man', as St John tersely puts it.

Nor can we imagine him either using or advocating the invariable use of 'loving' words. To speak the truth was obviously to him more important than to make his hearers comfortable: though, equally obviously, his genuine love for men gave him tact, wisdom, and sympathy.

He was love in action.

But he was not meek and mild.

✛

10 October

THE ADVENTURE

It is true that God is our 'refuge' but he is also our 'strength'.

The Christian life is essentially an adventure.

We have no right to pray 'Let me to thy bosom fly', when we should be out in God's strength fighting the dragons of evil in the world.

⁜

11 October

REFUGE AND STRENGTH

The authentic Christian tradition, and particularly the biographies of those who might be considered in the front rank of Christian 'saints', show that throughout the ages heroic men and women have found in God their 'refuge' as well as their 'strength'. It would be absurd to think that people of such spiritual stature were all under the influence of a childish regression. We are forced to look further for the explanation.

It has been well said by several modern psychologists that it is not the outward storms and stresses of life that defeat and disrupt personality, but its inner conflicts and miseries. If a man is happy and stable at heart, he can normally cope, even with zest, with difficulties that lie outside his personality.

Christians maintain that it is precisely this secure centre which faith in God provides. The genuine Christian can and does venture out into all kinds of exacting and even perilous activities, but all the time he knows that he has a completely stable and unchanging centre of operations to which he can return for strength, refreshment, and recuperation.

In that sense he does 'escape' to God, though he does not avoid the duties or burdens of life. His very 'escape' fits him for the day-to-day engagement with life's strains and difficulties.

12 October

CHURCHINESS

There are doubtless many reasons for the degeneration of Christianity into 'churchiness', and the narrowing of the Gospel for all mankind into a set of approved beliefs. But the chief cause must be the worship of an inadequate god, a cramped and regulated god who is 'a good churchman', according to the formulas of the worshipper.

For it is actual behaviour that reveals the real object of a man's worship.

✤

13 October

ILLS AND ACCIDENTS

In this experimental world, to which God has given the risky privilege of free will, there are inevitably 'ills and accidents'. Moreover, the cumulative effect over the centuries of millions of individuals choosing to please themselves rather than the Designer of 'the whole show' has infected the whole planet. That is what the theologians mean when they call this a 'sinful' world.

This naturally means that, so far as this world is concerned, the tough, insensitive, and selfish will frequently appear to get away with it, while the weak and sensitive will often suffer. Once we admit the possibilities of free will we can see that injustices and grievances are inevitable. (As Christ once said [Matthew 18:7], 'It *must needs be* that offences come.')

We may not agree with the risk that God took in giving man the power to choose. We might even have preferred God to have made a race of robots who were unfailingly good and cheerful and kind. But it is not in the least a question of what God *could have done*, but a question of what he *has done*.

We have to accept the scheme of things as it is. If we must blame someone, it is surely fairer to blame man who has chosen wrongly and so produced a world awry.

✛

14 October

CONSCIENCE

To many people conscience is almost all that they have by way of knowledge of God. This still, small voice which makes them feel guilty and unhappy before, during, or after wrongdoing, is God speaking to them.

It is this which, to some extent at least, controls their conduct. It is this which impels them to shoulder the irksome duty and choose the harder path.

No serious advocate of a real, adult religion would deny the function of conscience, or deny that its voice may at least give some inkling of the moral order that lies behind the obvious world in which we live. Yet to make conscience into God is a highly dangerous thing to do.

For one thing, as we shall see in a moment, conscience is by no means an infallible guide. For another, it is extremely unlikely that we shall ever be moved to worship, love, and serve a nagging inner voice that, at worst, spoils our pleasure and, at best, keeps us rather negatively on the path of virtue.

Conscience can be so easily perverted or morbidly developed in the sensitive person, and so easily ignored and silenced by the insensitive, that it makes a very unsatisfactory god.

15 October

THE VOICE WITHIN

There are many, even among professing Christians, who are made miserable by a morbidly developed conscience, which they quite wrongly consider to be the voice of God.

Many a housewife overdrives herself to please some inner voice that demands perfection. The voice may be her own demands or the relics of childhood training, but it certainly is not likely to be the voice of the Power behind the universe.

On the other hand, the middle-aged business man who has long ago taught his conscience to come to heel, may persuade himself that he is a good-living man. He may even say, with some pride, that he would never do anything against his conscience. But it is impossible to believe that the feeble voice of the half-blind thing which he calls conscience, is in any real sense the voice of God.

Neither the hectically over-developed nor the falsely-trained, nor the moribund conscience can ever be regarded as God, or even part of him. For if it is, God can be made to appear to the sensitive an over-exacting tyrant, and to the insensitive a comfortable accommodating 'voice within' which would never interfere with a man's pleasure.

16 October

POLES APART

Christ's approach to individuals was different in every case. If he on his own showing is 'meek and lowly in heart', we shall do well to follow his example.

If we are 'strong personalities' or 'powerful preachers' or 'every inch a vicar', it is only too possible for us never to be 'meek and lowly', never to hear what people are really thinking, never to under-stand what they are really feeling.

We may have a great following, we may make many proselytes, but I am not sure we bring men to God. It is not that we should change the eternal verities (how can we anyway?). It is that we do not begin to apply these verities until we have learned to love and understand people and until we have won their confidence.

Jesus used parables which were based on current modes of thought. We too have to learn the modes of thought in which our people are actually thinking.

They are poles apart as a rule from those of a theological student.

17 October

ON THE ROAD TO EMMAUS

If we are to understand the strange failure of the two walkers on the road to Emmaus to recognize the risen Christ, we must do some intelligent imagining.

It is easy enough for us, with the benefit of hindsight, to see the crucifixion as a triumph. But to those two it was an utter disaster. The man who was publicly executed was seen to die, and with that death came the heartbreaking desolation of disappointed hope and the anguish of intense personal loss.

They were completely obsessed with the shattering catastrophe and could think and talk of nothing else.

As they trudged along the seven-mile road, their eyes still red with weeping, their heads would be covered with the customary 'burnous'. This gave them some shield from the fierce heat of the westering sun, and made some little shelter from the reflected glare of the choking white dust at their feet.

Physically it would have been difficult to see and recognize another traveller, especially since, at the beginning of their encounter, he seemed to know nothing of the tragedy which filled their minds.

But there is another deeper reason for their failure to recognize Christ walking with them like any other dusty traveller. When human minds are faced with sudden and overwhelming tragedy people often cry 'No! No!', as if by denying what has plainly happened they are somehow stopping it from happening. Then, as the mind eventually accepts the worst, the grief becomes, temporarily at least, an obsession.

The heartbroken can, for the time, think of nothing else, and they can talk of nothing else. Over and over again the mind goes wearily round the same heartbreaking circle, thinking of what might have been and trying to make its adjustment to what cannot now be altered.

Luke, like any other good doctor, would know this.

❖

18 October

THE SPARK REKINDLED

I do not see any reason to suppose that the Greek word translated 'were holden' in St Luke's Emmaus story (Luke 24:13–35) denotes anything supernatural. The force of the word is that they were 'prevented' or 'inhibited' from recognizing their Companion.

This is how Luke, the Greek-speaking doctor, recorded their story. In English we should say more naturally, 'something prevented them from recognizing him'.

We could easily explain this by the purely physical causes of sheer fatigue, of sleeplessness and anxiety. We could truthfully say that they were walking in the late afternoon with 'the sun in their eyes'. Much more to the point is the psychological 'block' which intense grief may bring.

In certain circumstances, the grief-obsession excludes every other subject. With what kindly and gentle steps, Jesus led those despairing minds into acceptance of the divine wisdom, prophesied of old and now fulfilled by his own death and resurrection.

Small wonder that their hearts 'began to burn within them'!

But the rekindled spark of faith did not burst into flame until they were with him indoors, and they had heard the familiar words of blessing and received from his pierced hands the broken bread.

✤

19 October

BUT GOD...

When we were at school, we were told that the conjunction 'but' is used to introduce a contrasting idea. A sentence can go merrily enough, and then a 'but' comes in, and a different idea appears.

It is because the idea of God is a contrasting one that the writers of the Bible so often use that phrase, 'But God'. They write of the plans, the thoughts, the desires and the hopes of men, and again and again comes the word of contrast, 'But God...'

It is a contrasting idea because the men who wrote the Scriptures wrote from the spiritual point of view, and the lives of the men about whom they were writing were lived from man's point of view. Men thought and planned and hoped and feared without God, so that when their history came to be written from the spiritual—that is, the true—point of view, the words, 'But God...' are frequently interjected.

✤

20 October

SPIRITUAL BANKRUPTCY

This is an example of 'But God...' from that parable of Jesus which we call the parable of the rich fool.

231

Here was a man who had 'made his pile'. He had risen early and worked late, and now, he told himself, that the time had come for a little relaxation. Nothing very wrong in that, we may say, 'But God said, Thou fool!' He was called a fool because that very night his soul was to be required of him.

That does not necessarily mean that he was to die, but that he was to render spiritual account. True, his money bags were full of gold, and no one could say that he was a failure, but God calls him a fool because he is spiritually bankrupt.

A friend of mine once dreamed that he was stranded without friends in a foreign country. He was hungry and cold, and in need of a night's rest. His pockets were full of the money of the country which he had left behind, but no one would take it in the country in which he found himself.

A rather unpleasant nightmare, you will agree, but it was the actual predicament in which the rich man of the parable found himself. He had plenty of the riches of this world, but, when he stood before God, that wealth was not current.

It simply did not count. He found himself spiritually bankrupt.

What we are in the eyes of God is what we really are. Neither our balance in the bank, nor the letters before or after our name, will matter in the day that we face our God.

It will be a question then of what we really are—whether we have grown rich through faith in God and through self-giving service, or whether we have been so wrapped up in ourselves that we are spiritually bankrupt.

You see how the mention of God introduced a contrasting idea. 'But God...'

✣

21 October

THE KINDNESS OF GOD

One of the hardest tasks is to bring home to people the fact that God loves them. So many people look upon God as the Celestial Spy, a kind of Super Policeman, only interested in discovering their faults. But God, says St Paul, is not like that, and he tries an illustration.

Some of us, he says in effect, might be willing to give our lives for a man whose life was really valuable, *but God* commends his love, in that while we were yet sinners, Christ died for our sins.

You and I have all sorts of ideas of him—that he is capricious, exacting, tyrannical—but God, in actual fact, loved us when our hearts were estranged from him, and our minds were set against him.

An old gypsy woman, whose life had been hard and cruel, and whose husband was a drunken brute, lay dying in hospital. Those who had befriended her found it hard work to make her realize the love of God. To her, God was someone immensely powerful, but hard and unfeeling—a reflection of the blows and curses she had received during her life. However, as sometimes happens, as she drew near the gates of death, the veil was, as it were, drawn aside, and she was given a glimpse of that other world.

Those who had watched her said that a wonderful light came into her eyes, and an indescribable smile lighted up her face.

Her dying words were, 'But he is so kind!'

One of the things that will surprise us most in heaven will be the realization of the kindness of God.

You and I may have our wrong ideas about him, 'but God' is actually our truest and most loving Friend.

✣

22 October

THE HARD WAY

I was ordained to help to create and sustain faith, never to weaken or destroy it. That is why I wrote *Ring of Truth*. It was time someone spoke up for the reliability and historicity of the Christian faith.

I was born with no silver spoon in my mouth, ecclesiastical or otherwise. As I said earlier, I worked out my faith the hard way. I am not going to have a pearl of great price knocked out of anyone's hands by arguments which I wrestled with twenty-five years ago.

When I began my work of translating the New Testament, my chief object was to clarify obscurity and make the beautiful but archaic into the intelligible and relevant. But I had no idea of the sheer power of the deceptively simple Greek. The material is so alive that you must accept the challenge of its intrinsic authority, or leave it alone.

Most people, apparently, take the second course.

✣

23 October

THIS SUPERLATIVE MAN

Unless we believe in what we commonly call the 'incarnation'—that is, that God really became a human being in Jesus—the real significance of the crucifixion and the resurrection will always escape us.

But how could one human being be both Son of Man and Son of God?

What very often happens is that we worship and admire Christ as Son of God, and then draw back, out of very reverence, from applying to him the normal limitations of a man. Alternatively, we see so clearly the humanity of this superlative man that we forget that he was in a unique sense the Son of God, even God-in-human form.

The double truth is extremely hard for the human mind to understand, and yet it is the heart of our faith.

We shall never know, in the depths of our being, the meaning of the crucifixion, or of the triumph of the resurrection, until we see that this man Jesus was God being a man, and not in any sense God pretending to be a man.

As we meditate upon the eternal truths, concentrated and historically expressed on the first Good Friday and the first Easter Day, we should remember that we are watching a man, a man superlatively strong in spirit and constantly in touch with the Father (who is also our Father), but not at any time some demi-God or supernatural human being.

✣

24 October

WHAT DOES IT PROFIT...?

In the New Testament, there is no blinking the fact that this world is cruel and evil, and that nothing less than the power of the living God can alter the situation. New Testament writers plainly regard this little life as lived against a background of what, for want of a better word, we may call 'eternity'.

This is no 'pie in the sky' sentimentality. The very men who believed in the 'world to come' were the ones who worked the hardest and believed most strongly in the power of God to change men in the 'here and now'. If modern man is to be rescued from his despair, he must have the humility to accept this conviction of the early Christians. They were 'strangers and pilgrims' in this passing world but they did not regard it as a mere tiresome interlude to be endured before the everlasting joys that lay ahead.

I do not in the least despise the magnificent achievements of science, but it does not really help to travel faster than sound or to make any other technological advance if we isolate ourselves from the transforming power of God by our own self-sufficiency.

What, for example, does it profit a man to extend the span of his physical life on this earth if he altogether fails to make contact with the mind and heart of his Creator?

✛

25 October

THERE IS THE WORD!

This Word of God about which I believe we can be absolutely certain, and to which we can only respond through our faculty of faith, is more certain than anything else that we know by any other of our senses. It may be illogical, it may be non-provable, it may even seem nonsense to the unbeliever, but to the Christian it is not merely the confirmation of all his inklings and intuitions. *It is nothing less than certainty.*

For us this Word of God is, for the most part, focused in the recorded words of our Lord and in the inspired words of those who wrote the Epistles of the New Testament. I do not say that God did not give glimpses of truth before he sent his Son, nor do I say that he ceased to lead us into all truth when the apostles were all dead. What I believe is that this particular Christian certainty over the basic facts of our faith which so emboldened the early Church and made it like a triumphant rock in the surrounding pagan world, is to be rediscovered by us today in the acceptance of the New Testament itself.

The Word of God is there.

26 October

TRUE MATURITY

To be religious is, in the minds of many, babyish and immature. But exactly the reverse is true. It is the baby who yells with rage when he cannot get what he wants. It is the grown-up person who learns to control himself. It is the undeveloped man who cannot control his own desires and powers. It is the mature person who has learned to discipline himself and obey a Power higher than himself.

The adult human being is the one who has learned to deny his self-love and has turned his love outwards towards God and his neighbour.

Which are the things which we most admire and which move us most? They are courage and self-sacrificing love.

Why? Because these two qualities deliberately deny two of our most fundamental instincts, self-preservation and the desire to look after the self.

We can always hold out the Christian life as the truly mature one.

✣

27 October

MIDDLE AGE

One of the advantages of middle age is that you can look both backwards and forwards with a fair amount of sympathy and understanding. You can still remember what it was like to be young, and to be old appears to be, not, as it does to the very young, to belong almost to another race, but as a natural thing to be accepted. Furthermore you can, in middle age, having achieved a certain amount of experience and knowledge of life, look around and reflect upon what is worthwhile and what is not.

Meeting people in all sorts of troubles and difficulties, as I constantly do, I cannot help being appalled at the number who have nothing to hold on to when times are difficult, and who lack any sense of living life in harmony with a purpose.

It appears to me that the great message of Christianity to the present generation is to proclaim that sense of purpose. Life is meant to be a much more satisfying experience than merely enduring or enjoying each incident as it comes along.

It is surely meant to be nothing less than co-operating with God's purpose—a co-operation which means that we change from being little self-centred individuals into people who know and love God.

❖

28 October

MORE THAN CONQUERORS

The sharing of common danger is not comparable with the persecution of a minority. Yet the spells of acute danger which we endured in wartime brought home to us the magnificent and joyful resilience of early Christianity.

I can remember, for example, a particularly dangerous time, when we were officially urged not to have large groups of people assembled together. I used to conduct short services in people's houses or in air-raid shelters. Again and again passages from Paul's letters could scarcely have been more apt.

One particular truth I tried to see then, and urged others to accept, is contained in Paul's words: 'in all these things we are more than conquerors' (Romans 8:37).

We often think that eventually all will be well (and so it will), but Paul's point is that *in the midst of cold and hunger, of danger to life and limb, we are more than conquerors*.

29 October

'IT ISN'T FAIR...'

We all accept, at least with part of our minds, the parable of the prodigal son. We think it only right and fair that the ungrateful and spendthrift son should 'fill his belly with the husks that the swine did eat'. 'Fair's fair,' we say. But what is fair about the father running towards the returning prodigal and, before he could complete his carefully prepared speech of penitence, falling on his neck and kissing him, dressing him up in fine clothes and jewellery, and ordering food and a dance in his honour? It is just not fair, as the elder brother was quick to point out, but *it is a picture of the love of God which is unconditional and utterly generous*.

God loves because that is his nature. However hard it may be for us to grasp this, we must do it, or we will not understand what God is and does.

'It was even while we were dead in sins, his enemies, alienated from the life of God, that he loved us and all men—for God so loved the world.'

When this basic certainty that God is love is grasped by our faculty and spreads into both heart and mind, it brings with it a joyous certainty.

God *so* loved the world...!

30 October

A CONSUMING FIRE

How far removed from the New Testament are the insipid words of the hymn which says 'he came sweet influence to impart, a gracious willing guest', and goes on to say, 'and his that gentle voice we hear, soft as the breath of even, that checks each fault, that calms each fear…'

Anyone who has any experience at all of the living God knows that he is nothing at all like this somebody who tut-tuts politely at our failings and lays a soothing hand upon our anxious little heads.

The God who lives in us if we allow him, is not necessarily always gentle. He can be wind and fire and a whole lot of other things.

He can give us strength, but he can also show us our weakness!

He will 'increase our faith', but frequently not in the way we want or expect.

He will show us, as we can bear it, more and more truth, but he will shatter our illusions without scruple, perhaps especially illusions about ourselves.

He will give us moments of wonderful perception, but will also allow us to endure terrifying darkness. He is indeed all goodness and light but he will show no more compunction towards the evil things that we have allowed to grow in our hearts than a human surgeon would to a malignant growth.

The men of old were hardly exaggerating when they said, 'Our God is a consuming fire' (Hebrews 12:29).

31 October

GOD-DEFICIENCY

Many people of sensitivity and perception, whether they have a religious faith or not, view with dismay the growing materialism of this age. To anyone who is the least alive to the contemporary God, the general life of this country, despite many virtues, exhibits all the symptoms of God-deficiency. For the present generation is, albeit unconsciously, attempting to prove that man can live by bread alone.

'The good life' is conceived almost entirely in terms of creature comforts, labour-saving appliances, better clothes, better and longer holidays, more money to spend and more leisure to enjoy.

None of these things is wrong in itself. But when they are assumed to satisfy every desire, ambition and aspiration of man, we are surely right to be alarmed at the grip of materialism.

For when possessions, pleasures and the thought of physical security fill a man's horizon, he ceases to ask himself such basic questions as 'What am I?' or 'What am I here for?'

Modern man can and may gain the whole world. But he will lose his soul.

Let your attitude to life be that of Christ Jesus himself. For he, who had always been God by nature, did not cling to his privileges as God's equal, but stripped himself of every advantage by consenting to be a slave by nature and being born a man. And plainly seen as a human being, he humbled himself by living a life of utter obedience, to the point of death, and the death he died was the death of a common criminal. That is why God has now lifted him to the heights, and has given him the name beyond all names, so that at the name of Jesus 'every knee shall bow', whether in heaven or earth or under the earth. And that is why 'every tongue shall confess' that Jesus Christ is Lord, to the glory of God the Father.

PHILIPPIANS 2:5–11

November

In my opinion, whatever we may have to go through now is less than nothing compared with the magnificent future God has in store for us. The whole creation is on tiptoe to see the wonderful sight of the sons of God coming into their own. The world of creation cannot as yet see reality, not because it chooses to be blind, but because in God's purpose, it has been so limited—yet it has been given hope. And the hope is that, in the end, the whole of created life will be rescued from the tyranny of change and decay, and have its share in that magnificent liberty which can only belong to the children of God!

ROMANS 8:18–21

✛

1 November

WHEN DEPRESSED…

I have suffered from ill-health during the last few years. To a large extent this was my own fault, for I accepted hundreds of demands on my time which were out of all proportion to my real strength. I should have realized that sooner or later a reaction was bound to set in. Therefore, I must say briefly that I now know a great deal about the assorted darknesses and depressions that can afflict the human spirit. And I know very well indeed how faith in oneself and one's own integrity, let alone faith in an omnipotent God, can be severely shaken and tested.

Of one thing I am quite certain. There is nothing that can help a man through the lengthy period of recovery better than a sustained faith in God, whatever one's feelings may happen to be.

I have read a great deal during the last few years, but I have never discovered anything that even remotely helps those who have to endure such times of depression unless it be found in, or derived from, the teachings of Jesus Christ and the New Testament generally.

✤

2 November

FRIENDS

Friends have helped in my period of depression, but I have to say, in all honesty, chiefly those who have themselves suffered. And what are they but agents of the living God? I cannot bring myself to say that 'suffering' is, by itself, a good thing. Yet it remains mysteriously true that those who have, through faith, conquered or come to terms with suffering are the only ones who can either understand or offer constructive help.

To go into all the implications of what I have hinted at here would require a book, and I doubt if I should ever be competent to write it.

But I see no hope at all in any view of life but the Christian one.

✤

3 November

SPIRITUAL HEALING

Jesus was in many cases able to get to the storm-centre of the mental or physical disturbance and resolve it with authoritative love.

We do not know even yet how far the mind affects the body or the body the mind, or how far either of them is influenced by spiritual power—by intercessory prayer, for example. We know how to 'cure' certain diseases with fair accuracy, but what we are really doing is removing the obstacles which are preventing a natural ability to heal itself which both the human body and mind possess.

It does not seem to be in the least unreasonable that a man of concentrated spiritual power should be able to remove these obstacles instantaneously.

The whole business of 'spiritual' healing is a much debated one, and I do not propose to enter any controversy here. I am simply concerned to record my own conviction that the miracles of healing which Jesus performed were perfectly genuine, even though they may be described in the jargon of the day.

✤

4 November

THE INNER SELF

I believe that a 'theology of the inner self' (a thought I take from Harry Williams' book *The True Wilderness*) might answer several very important questions. What is it, for example, that lives within the spirit of a man which enables him to detect truth, even though it may prove painful and destructive to his previous illusions?

What God-given faculty is it that enables us to recognize the Word of God as the Word of God and not as a mere human opinion or doctrine?

From my own experience, that is from my own knowledge of my own inner truth, I believe this recognition of God's words to be a valid part of human experience. And when I find, as I have done over the last thirty years, that this inner experience is shared by thousands in various parts of the world, I am convinced that here is an authentic part of human existence which is all too often ignored.

It is not so much that the bare Word speaks to us from the New Testament out of context (although, of course, it sometimes does that), as that what God has to say through the inspired writers sheds quite a unique light upon human living and dying.

✢

5 November

REASSURANCE

We have grown away from the idea—and rightly, in my judgment—that Jesus Christ is, to put it crudely, the 'cushion' between the angry Father and us sinful beings. There can be no schizophrenia in the nature of God; and in any case, the ascended Christ had made the reconciliation which we could never make.

Behind these mysterious and dreadful words, 'He hath made him to be sin for us, who knew no sin' (2 Corinthians 5:21) and 'He should taste death for every man' (Hebrews 2:9), there lies more than a hint of the personal cost of our redemption. But at the time of the ascension this was over; the agony, the darkness and the dereliction of Calvary had been endured, and the resurrection was the proof that the work was done.

What now remained for the ascended Christ to do?

✢

6 November

THE TRANSFIGURATION

There is a good deal in the New Testament about light and darkness, and I think we should constantly remind ourselves to what an extent we take artificial light for granted.

Most of us live within touch of an electric light switch, many of us live in cities and towns whose streets and houses are illuminated, and the electric torch operated by a battery is a commonplace almost all over the world.

We thus find in the world of the first century AD that light creates a much greater impression of divine presence or divine happening than speed or size or physical power, which are the things which impress many of us today.

The story of the transfiguration is a particularly good example of this. The dazzling brightness of both the face of Jesus and of his clothes filled Peter, James and John with awe as did the sight of Moses and Elijah talking to Jesus.

It seems to me it would be quite possible to relate the incident in a different way. Suppose that the limitations of time and earthly life were, so to speak, momentarily lifted. Peter, James and John would then see Jesus radiantly bright talking without the slightest sense of anachronism with the two men of the past who represented the law and the prophets. Thus one could say not so much that Jesus was transfigured but that the disciples were temporarily relieved of their earth-blindness.

It must have been an ecstatic experience and one which Peter, quite understandably, but in a rather clumsy way, wanted to prolong.

Once again to me it bears the hallmark of a true happening, however shortly and naïvely described.

✥

7 November

THE MILLSTONE

All cruelty is bad, not merely for the victim but for the perpetrator. Christians are right to protest wherever they can against any form of cruelty.

Some of the sternest words Christ ever uttered were directed against those who were cruel to children. But sometimes I think the fierceness of his anger is blunted by the familiar beauty of the Authorized Version. Do you remember, for instance, what he said about a man 'who should offend one of these little ones'? He said, 'It were better for that man that a millstone were hung about his neck and he were cast into the sea' (Mark 9:42).

But do you see what he is really saying? The 'gentle Jesus meek and mild' is saying that it would be better for a man to die a violent and painful death than to assault or exploit one little child!

Those are words that should make us think.

❖

8 November

CRUELTY

Cruelty to people, and especially to children, is a far more important question than cruelty to animals. I cannot forget that Hitler was very fond of dogs, or that I have known animal-lovers who would sit up all night with a sick dog, but who showed little or no love to their own families.

It is comparatively easy for most decent people to love animals. Nearly always they are grateful and responsive, and our love is returned. But loving people is different. It is costly and difficult. Our love may be rejected. The good we try to do may be misinterpreted.

Do not suppose that I am indifferent to the suffering of animals. We have Christ's own words that not a sparrow falls to the ground without the knowledge of the Father in heaven. Man is undoubtedly meant to live in this world as a son of God, and that means treating the lesser animal creation as God's creatures, never to be despised or exploited or caused unnecessary suffering. But, again on Christ's authority, a human being is worth many sparrows.

I sometimes wish that some of the love so freely given to dogs and cats and canaries could be given to human beings who so desperately need it.

9 November

DUMB BLONDES

'Of course,' said the fat man, leaning against the bar, in a film of the 'thirties, 'I like dumb blondes. In fact,' he went on, pushing his glass across for a refill, 'the dumber they are the better I like 'em.'

There was a murmur of agreement.

The fat man might have gone a bit further. What he would really like would be a race of glamorous blondes, altogether charming and attractive, who would give him all the pleasure and thrill he wanted without his ever having to think that they might have minds—or even souls. He really wants his females to be living *things*, but not real people. And of course his attitude produces the female reply to that sort of thing—the gold-digger (as they used to say).

Most of the miseries of this world are caused by this habit—treating people as things, not people.

✛

10 November

PEOPLE MATTER

The employer who uses his employees as machines, the parent who regards his children as his own possessions, the young people who treat their home as simply a cheap hotel, the attractive girl who looks at all men as mere tributes to her sex-appeal—they are all trying to use people as things instead of recognizing them as people.

It is a vicious circle! The fat man produces the gold-digger, the inhuman employer produces the clock-watcher, the possessive parent the thankless child, and so on *ad infinitum*. The world is full of it.

What is obviously wanted is something that will make people see each other and treat each other as people who matter, instead of exploiting them as things to be made use of.

Jesus taught that this could be done if men would do two simple, though difficult, things.

First, recognize that there is a God who is equally the Father of everyone, fat man, blonde, parent, employer, employee, and all the rest, and give him a wholehearted loyalty.

Secondly, treat other people exactly as you would wish to be treated yourself. In other words to love your neighbour as yourself.

He also said that the Spirit needed to effect this change is immediately available to those who mean business.

⁂

11 November

A FELLOWSHIP OF HOPE

The English poet Swinburne, probably feeling that Victorian piety had taken away the joy and colour from life, wrote these bitter words about Christ:

> *Thou hast conquered, O pale Galilean;*
> *the world has grown grey from Thy breath.*

But if Swinburne had studied the history of the Church immediately following the death of the 'pale Galilean', he would have found exactly the reverse was true. The surrounding world was indeed grey, sometimes black with corruption and all kinds of evil, but in the young Church there was gay and indomitable hope.

Nothing could quench this hope, for these men and women now knew for certain that death had largely become sodden with self-indulgence.

The brave, new fellowship of believers in Christ was a light and a flame in the darkness.

It was the fellowship of hope.
It is a good thought on this Remembrance day.

✤

12 November

WIDE OPEN TO GOD

It is well worth our while to study the leading characteristics of New Testament Christians. These men and women, when all is said and done, were as human as we are. God cannot conceivably have changed in his nature or purpose over the centuries, but we may find as we compare the life-attitude of New Testament Christians with our own that a subtle but disastrous change has come over us in the intervening centuries. We may find that our timidity and rigidity, our prejudices and preconceived ideas, are most effectively blocking the purpose of God.

We must take the risk of being wide open on the Godward side.

✤

13 November

DUTY PERFORMANCE

Many Christians are consciously or unconsciously on the defensive. They are only too well aware that they are a small minority, and many of them are faithfully and strenuously defending their convictions.

Their courage and loyalty to Christ in the face of the widespread apathy of the surrounding world is wholly admirable. But, with some notable exceptions, the Christian faith is only being maintained within existing churches, and is not spreading very far beyond actual church membership.

However much we love the Church, we have to admit that, though it may exhibit the quieter and more inconspicuous virtues, it is very rarely making any considerable impact upon the modern pattern of living. It has unquestionably lost power, and it has lost vision. The worst aspect is that the Christian faith itself is being reduced to a dreary duty-performance which, to say the least of it, is most unattractive.

14 November

BECOMING

In my own experience, limited as it may be, the glorious certainty of the early Church has been replaced today by a kind of wavering hopefulness, by no means free from attempts at self-justification.

If we are to recapture the buoyancy and vigour of New Testament Christians, we must stop quibbling about the question of our own forgiveness and our own standing with God.

We must accept the generosity of God, and stand upright as his sons and daughters.

The attitude of New Testament letters, in general, is never one of dwelling upon man's sinfulness (even though it was sometimes necessary to remind people of what they were), but an encouraging looking forward to what they might *become through the grace and power of God*.

15 November

SELLING RELIGION

I remember once sharing lodgings with a commercial traveller. He said to me one day, 'You know, Padre, I don't envy you your job.'

I was naturally interested and asked him why. He replied, 'Well, my job is to sell radio sets, which most people want; but your job is to sell religion and I should imagine that is pretty hard work.'

'Selling religion' is perhaps a crude way of describing my job, but it is true that a large part of my work lies in 'getting across' the Christian religion to ordinary men and women, and particularly, for some years, to young people.

We must be clear in our minds what it is we want to do in teaching the Christian religion especially to young people. It is not for us to impose our own ideas and beliefs upon young and impressionable minds. If we ourselves have strong personalities we shall be tempted to do this, that is to impose religion from the outside, as it were, and we shall meet with a certain superficial success. But it will not last. When our personal influence is removed from the youngster's life, we shall find, to our sorrow, that the religion we tried to implant was, in fact, merely imposed by our stronger personality.

Our real objective is far harder. It is to inspire and foster within the youngster's own personality a right relation towards God and his neighbour, a spirit of willing co-operation with the great Reality that we call God.

✤

16 November

STAND ASIDE!

I have known churches where the preacher, by his exceptionally strong personality, packed his church. But when the time came for him to leave, most of the people left the church also!

What appeared to be a success in the spiritual realm was really only the success of a strong personality.

What we all have to learn to do, whether we be parsons or laymen, is not to use our personalities to draw people to ourselves but, as it were, to stand aside and let them be drawn to the Master whom we serve.

This is not an easy lesson to learn by any means, for it is very flattering to our pride to be admired and imitated.

But if we are out for real, as distinct from superficial results, we need to watch our step just here.

✣

17 November

PARABLE

A good story will often hold attention and point a useful lesson. You can sense the attention of young people relaxing the moment you begin to say, 'Now the meaning of that story for us is...'

Be sure that your story is true, and if possible check its source. A lot of harm may result if a boy or girl subsequently discovers that a story told as true was really fiction.

There is, of course, no harm in telling a fictitious story as long as we preface it with some remark as 'Now this story is not true'.

The good modern parable is useful for the same reason that parables were useful in the days when Christ used them. You may have wondered why he did so. The reason is that anybody, old or young, will listen to a story, and while their interest is held, their defences, so to speak, are unguarded, so that the lesson of the parable can get into the heart of the hearer. That is why we must beware of pointing the moral, for at once the defences go up again.

You will never find Jesus Christ, after a most telling parable, that of the prodigal son, for instance, saying, 'Now the moral of this story is...'

He let the truth do its own work.

❖

18 November

HUNGRY FOR BEAUTY

I once spent a fortnight giving a camp holiday to some boys from one of London's worst slums. These boys, when they arrived, were dirty, undisciplined, noisy and unpleasant in every way, but after only ten days the change in them was almost miraculous. Their behaviour, cleanliness and even manners, improved beyond all knowledge.

It became pathetically obvious that their noisy Cockney toughness had been nothing but a crude defence against the dreadful conditions under which they had been living.

It may surprise you to learn that these boys received the truths of the Christian religion in many cases with obvious emotion.

It seemed as if their souls, quite unknown to themselves, were hungry for the beauty and love and ideals that Christianity could give.

❖

19 November

LAUGH!

God does not wait for our perfection before he can use us in his purpose, a fact for which we can be grateful. Let us, without being complacent or self-indulgent, come to good-humoured terms with ourselves.

It is a good thing to see how far we are off course, but no good purpose is served by despising ourselves for having been such poor pilots.

It is a strange thing how hard it is for most of us to laugh at ourselves. We would far rather despise ourselves as sinners, even the chief of sinners, than laugh at ourselves as self-important little idiots!

The plank in our eye probably provoked the angels to a good deal of laughter, but in our precious dignity, we would rather have orgies of contrition and repentance and self-loathing than the healthy gust of one good-humoured laugh at ourselves.

✢

20 November

NO SECRET

The defenders of the jargon and phrases of the Church's traditions hold that there must of necessity be a specialized vocabulary, just as there is in any other specialized form of human activity, whether it is music, architecture or electronic engineering.

This is a thoroughly unsound argument, for Christ did not come into the world to bring men 'specialized activity', but life, fuller and more satisfying than it had ever been before.

If the churches have made Christianity appear to be some kind of specialized spiritual performance, so much the worse for them. The real purpose of Christ, the real relevance of the Gospel, is surely to enable men to live together as sons of God.

Human beings, like children, love to have secrets, love to be 'in the know'. But the Christian religion was never meant to be a secret recipe for living, held by a few. It is Good News for all mankind. Because it is that, the more clearly and intelligibly it can be presented, the more faithfully it is following its Master's purpose.

✢

21 November

FREEDOM

Christ said that he came to make man free. He taught not only that there are certain unseen laws behind life which can't be safely ignored, but also that there is a new technique of living by which men learn to be free.

Those who have taken the trouble to learn this say that he was right. They find they are free to be and do what in their secret hearts they had always hoped that they were capable of being and doing. They find this is real freedom, whatever the external circumstances may be.

You can, of course, ignore the rules and refuse to learn the technique till your dying day. No one will stop you. But you won't find freedom— only frustration and that ridiculous infantile wish at the back of your mind, 'Oh, I do wish I could be free to do what I like!'

⁜

22 November

BY DAY

Night seems to be the usual time for ghosts to walk. You do not often hear of anyone seeing a ghost on a blazing summer afternoon. The spirits seem to prefer the shadows of the night.

Perhaps that is because people can't be quite sure what they do see then, and fatigue has made them rather more susceptible to suggestion. Besides, most of us give our imagination a little play in the evenings and keep our matter-of-factness for working hours.

Maybe that explains why we never hear of a séance being held in bright sunshine in the open air. Mediums say they must have the right 'atmosphere', and that usually means a darkened room, a ring of clasped hands and not too much scepticism present; otherwise the spirits can't get through.

All this makes it all the more remarkable that when the Man did come back from the dead it was all so free from 'spookiness', and most of the action took place in daylight in the open air.

But perhaps he did it deliberately, just to show that this was the real thing.

✛

23 November

FROM WOMB TO TOMB

Paul has a tremendous sense of the eternal world before which this little life is enacted. To him, heaven was not, as it would appear to the Victorians, a reward for being a good boy, but the vast illimitable, incomparable magnificence of true life.

At a time when all the social and economic emphasis is from 'womb to tomb', it is salutary to remember that all that happens from womb to tomb is a mere nothing compared with the glory that shall be revealed in us.

It is easy to scoff at this 'other-worldly' point of view.

My experience convinces me of the absolute necessity of this dimension.

✛

24 November

WORDS, WORDS, WORDS...

Think of the thousands of words that meet our ears through conversation, the radio and the cinema, and the thousands more that meet our eyes in the newspapers, magazines and books. The combined influence of this battery of words must be very considerable even to those who think they are strong-minded enough to hold their own opinions whatever anybody else may say or write.

We need to be thoroughly on our guard against the influence of words, particularly if the people who speak or write them have a particular axe to grind!

One of the best ways of avoiding being unduly influenced by words, and of keeping a proper sense of proportion, is getting into touch with God by prayers. Part of prayer (once we have got past the baby stage of thinking that it is just asking God for things), is the quiet thinking out of life's problems and perplexities in his presence, allowing his Spirit to steady and strengthen us as well as guide us, while we try to think things out as adult responsible people. Things get into their right proportions. Other things appear to us as false and pretentious, or even downright pompous and ridiculous when we look at them in the presence of Almighty God.

One of the beauties of being a Christian is that we have something of 'the mind of Christ'—and *he* was never slow to see through humbug or laugh at mere pretentiousness, however solemn and respectable it appeared.

✠

25 November

ALL TOGETHER

Vastly improved methods of communication and travel have meant the end of a safe, complacent 'parochial' outlook. Even if we try to detach ourselves personally from the world's burdens, we are assailed by newspapers, radio, and television, and we can scarcely help feeling something of the world's pains and problems.

This is by no means bad, for it means for the very first time in human history a great many intelligent men and women are realizing how interdependent we are as human beings. Nations, even whole continents, are awakening from the sleep of centuries, and while violent nationalism flares up from time to time, there is a growing sense among responsible people of all nations that we are 'all in it together'.

If we are to have hope amidst all the menaces and threats of today's world, it has got to be a sturdy and well-founded hope.

There can never be a return to the shallow optimism of those whose outlook was both narrow and complacent.

✛

26 November

GENUINE RELIGION

There is always a danger of 'religion' becoming over-complicated. Ceremonies which are meant to be acted parables of deep religious truth become so elaborate that the ceremony itself hides the truth it is meant to represent. It is only too easy to 'go through' the ceremonies and forget that the heart of religion is expressed in the quality of life.

In both Old and New Testaments, men have to be told that actual conduct is what matters. James said it too. 'Religion that is pure and genuine in the sight of God the Father will show itself by such things as visiting orphans and widows in their distress, and keeping oneself uncontaminated by the world' (James 1:27).

'He hath shewed thee, O man, what is good; and what doth the Lord require of thee, but to do justly, and to love mercy, and to walk humbly with thy God' (Micah 6:6–8).

It is really as simple as that!

✛

27 November

PORTRAIT OF GOD

Every man who has longed to know what God is like must sympathize with Philip. If only we could know what sort of person God really is, with how much more confidence, cheerfulness and courage we could face this business of living! Jesus declares plainly (John 14:6–10) that seeing him is the same thing as seeing the Father.

This naturally does not mean that the whole of God's infinity could be compressed into one human being. But it does mean that whenever we look at Jesus Christ we are looking at the character of God himself.

It is of the highest importance that we should 'see' Christ, and refuse to hold in our minds any conception of God which is incompatible with his character.

To see him, we need to read and think about him, and, since he himself is the road, the truth and the life, live spiritually close to him.

✣

28 November

THE BATTLE RAGES

Anyone who has ever tried to formulate a private prayer in silence, and in his own heart, will know what I mean by diabolical interference. The forces of evil are in opposition to the will of God. And the nearer a man approaches God's will, the more apparent and stronger and more formidable this opposition is seen to be. It is only when we are going in more or less the same direction as the devil that we are unconscious of any opposition at all.

These words by David Bolt are completely true to my own experience of life and to that of my Christian friends and correspondents.

The battle of which the New Testament speaks so realistically is still raging, and every Christian finds himself involved in it.

This is one more reason why these ancient writings ring so true in modern ears.

✣

29 November

WHY LOVE IS LACKING

A strange inhibition seems to have cramped and silenced many Christians. Because of the revelations of science (which surely can only increase our awe at the complex wisdom of our Creator), because of the so-called 'new theology', because of the oppressive weight of modern competitive materialism, people have frequently said that the word 'God' has lost its meaning.

They can, they say, no longer find it useful in communicating the Gospel.

I seriously doubt this. I have in years of pastoral work only occasionally found the word or the idea of 'God' irrelevant.

It is true that our conception of the vast mystery of 'God' is a million times greater than that of our forefathers.

It is true that much childish thinking, pious platitude and useless accretion must ruthlessly be thrown away.

It is obviously not good pretending that we live in the first century AD.

But neither is it any good pretending that human nature has 'come of age' and no longer needs the power of God to transform, to strengthen and to inspire.

It is no coincidence that the frightening lack of love which surrounds us in today's world goes hand in hand with a failure to believe in a personal God.

✤

30 November

TWO VIEWS

To show up the contrast between what Christ said and what is commonly thought, here are the two points of view:

Most people think:
- Happy are the 'pushers': for they get on in the world.
- Happy are the hard-boiled: for they never let life hurt them.
- Happy are they who complain: for they get their own way in the end.
- Happy are the blasé: for they never worry over their sins.
- Happy are the slave-drivers: for they get results.

- Happy are the knowledgeable men of the world: for they know their way around.
- Happy are the troublemakers: for they make people take notice of them.

Jesus said:
- How happy are the humble-minded, for the kingdom of heaven is theirs!
- How happy are those who know what sorrow means, for they shall be given courage and comfort.
- Happy are those who claim nothing, for the whole earth shall belong to them!
- Happy are those who are hungry and thirsty for goodness, for they will be fully satisfied!
- Happy are the merciful, for they will have mercy shown to them.
- Happy are the utterly sincere, for they will see God!
- Happy are those who make peace, for they will be known as sons of God!

Many people are trying the first recipe, and the result is a world full of unhappiness, greed, cruelty and selfishness. If, as Christians believe, the way that Jesus recommended is the right one, recommended by the expert in living, then that is not surprising.

✢

We pray that you will be strengthened from God's glorious power, so that you may be able to pass through any experience and endure it with joy. You will be able to thank the Father because you are privileged to share the lot of the saints who are living in the light. For he rescued us from the power of darkness, and re-established us in the kingdom of his beloved Son. For it is by him that we have been redeemed and have had our sins forgiven.

COLOSSIANS 1:11–14

December

For it is Christ Jesus as Lord whom we preach, not ourselves; we are your servants for Jesus' sake. God who first ordered light to shine in darkness has flooded our hearts with his light, so that we can enlighten men with the knowledge of the glory of God, as we see it in the face of Christ.

2 CORINTHIANS 4:5–6

✣

1 December

THE ARRIVED

I have taken over 5,000 funerals. Though, of course, many of the mourners on such occasions have a very sketchy faith, even in the case of those who are convinced Christians of some years standing, I find a strange inability to grasp the transitory nature of our present life and the breathtaking magnificence of the life which is to come.

I have, for instance, frequently suggested that it would be more appropriate to refer to the one whose physical body has died as the 'arrived' rather than the 'departed'.

No doubt there is nothing particularly original about this, but the significance lies in the fact that to many Christian people this is quite a new thought! They simply have not considered, or so it appears, that we are living this painful and difficult life against a background of unimaginable splendour.

Most of them hold desperately to a belief of some kind of survival, but that 'the sufferings of this present time are not worthy to be compared with the glory that shall be revealed in us' seems hardly to have entered their hearts and minds.

✤

2 December

THE NEW VISION

I don't know what sort of picture of himself a man like Matthew had, but I should think he saw himself as 'a dog with a bad name', a traitor to his own country, or one who was hated and despised and with all the possibilities of creative good long left behind. He probably saw himself as a man money-grabbing for the rest of his life. But when he met Christ, a new mental picture of himself came to life.

We can only guess here but I should think that, when Christ called him, he saw a possibility of a very different Matthew, redeemed and changed and re-empowered for good by the friendship of this Man.

Matthew's imagination was fired.

He arose and followed him.

That was the sort of thing Jesus was constantly doing. Men and women who had lost their self-respect and whose mental picture of themselves was a bitter cynical expectation of further degradation and misery, saw in him a new vision of themselves made new and clean.

They saw themselves loved... and worth something in God's world, and the willpower that had been weakened by long self-indulgence, was quickened by the power of this new vision.

They too followed him.

It is not much the present or even the immediate future that worries us but the *past*. The constant failures of the past make a barrier that no effort of will can ever surmount. The mental picture we have of ourselves is black and hopeless and that makes our actions black and hopeless too.

What is needed is not a further effort of will but a new vision of what we might be.

3 December

AUTO-SUGGESTION

There are many who have failed again and again, because, inwardly, they were dogged by past failure. They need not be. For 'I make all things new,' says Christ.

'If any man be in Christ, he is a new creation,' echoes St Paul. 'Old things are passed away, all things are new.'

The sheer newness of the vision makes life anew, with fresh possibilities, fresh adventures, fresh horizons.

Do you remember Saul Kane in the 'Everlasting Mercy'?

The whole world was washed clean for him, for a new vision of a new Saul Kane had gripped him. Christ can give us all a similar vision. You can be reconciled with God. Old things pass away. A new world opens before us, a world made possible by the enabling of his divine Companionship.

Paul knew the secret of successful auto-suggestion when he said long ago, 'I can do all things through Christ who strengtheneth me.'

4 December

'FOLLOW ME!'

The use of standards to produce a sense of sin should be effected with the utmost caution. You have only to raise the standard to reduce the finest Christian to a feeling of utter discouragement. We need to remember that 'ideals encourage but fantasies paralyse'.

I remember a man, a famous Keswick preacher, reducing his congregation to pulp by insisting on them being 'dead to the flesh'. After this effort he ate the largest supper I have seen eaten by anybody! This seemed to me a remarkable feat for a man who had just claimed that his flesh was utterly dead upon the cross of Christ.

Christ's method of saying 'Follow me' even to the most unlikely people is the real 'way in'. If we can present to people the living Christ who is saying to them, 'Follow me' even in the midst of their muddle and selfishness and bewilderment, there will be some who will follow him.

Their 'conviction of sin' can take care of itself.

After all, anyone who follows Christ for long will soon realize his weakness, cowardice and self-love.

✣

5 December

PRAYING AND PRAISING

In Paul's famous recipe for peace of mind, which is recorded for us in Philippians 4:6, he recommends a very close connection between praying and praising, between asking God for what we need and thanking him for what he has done.

Would you not agree with me that we are ready enough with our requests but rather slow, even downright mean, about our thanksgiving?

Quite apart from common courtesy to him it is extremely good *for us* to 'thank God'. It reminds us of what God has done in the past (which we all too easily forget), and brings its own encouragement by reminding us of what God eternally *is*.

Our moods may change and our circumstances may vary, but God is always the same, persistent unremitting love.

To thank him with an honest heart reminds us of the kind of God we worship.

6 December

THE PROBLEM OF GOODNESS

One of the problems which any thoughtful person will meet in the world is, strangely enough, the problem of goodness! You are bound to ask yourself why such stress should be laid upon churchgoing, praying, Bible-reading, and so on, in forming a good character if certain men and women are good, kind, honest and unselfish without any religious faith whatever!

In trying to answer the problem which this phenomenon raises, we must look more closely at it.

First, if it were possible to examine the antecedents of these good men and women, it would almost certainly be found that somewhere along the line of their development there was the influence of practising Christians. The good men and women themselves may have rejected the faith, but in all probability they owe their virtues to those who practised the faith a generation or so before.

Further, the great weakness of the men and women without faith is that they can have nothing to say to those who are not good by nature or temperament except, 'Why can't you be like me?'

They have no Gospel to give and no faith to share.

7 December

'CHRIST IS EVERYTHING!'

No one could say that Paul was 'disobedient to the heavenly vision'. Every energy of mind and body was devoted to the task of speeding the Good News. Despite every kind of humiliation, hardship, peril and pain, he pressed on.

He could have argued, if he had thought it worthwhile. Paul not only knew the philosophies and arguments of learned men, but he saw, with his own eyes, the sterility and impotence of any system of thought which ignores Christ.

Christ *is* everything.

He is God shown to us in human form.

He is God dying a criminal's death to reconcile men to himself. He is God triumphing over death. He is God entering men's hearts and transforming them from within—a thing unknown in a pagan world either then or now.

To Paul, God has entered the stream of human history *in person*.

He can never henceforth argue as though such an event had never happened.

✣

8 December

THE GOOD NEWS

The testimony of the New Testament cannot be lightly disregarded, nor can the claim of Christ be airily dismissed. Many otherwise intelligent people have never read with adult attention either the four Gospels or the letters of the New Testament.

The reliable historicity of the true fact of Christmas was in the early days often witnessed to in retrospect. But through the centuries, including our own, men have found that Jesus Christ is alive, ready to cleanse, inspire, and strengthen their own personalities.

As they have found him to be a real person, they have found his teachings true, his promises trustworthy, and this scheme of building a Kingdom of God an infinitely satisfying plan with which to co-operate.

It may be only then that there dawns upon us the true significance of the original, quiet, and simple Christmas story—and each Advent season, it takes our breath away. For human beings no longer exist in insignificance and fear on a lonely, whirling planet floating in terrifying space, while God, if he exists, is far away in some other dimension. *God has become Man!*

From henceforth God and Man are indissolubly linked.

God has not only made his personal visit, not only given us the pattern of true and happy living, not only died to reconcile us to himself, not only is risen again both to shatter the fear of death and to prove his own claims, but there is no barrier now between him and us. God in Christ is our contemporary.

If that is not Good News, it would be difficult to know what is!

❖

9 December

BEGIN AGAIN!

It is not good news for a man to be told that he is a hell-deserving sinner. It *is* good news for him to be told that he need no longer feel guilty and afraid towards God, and can begin here and now to live as God's son.

The stimulation of the guilt-sense in sensitive people can never be the proclamation of good news. Neither can the attempt to perpetrate an image of God who is either church-bound or Bible-bound, or both, be good news. Such distortions cause untold damage to the human spirit, and create a dozen rebels for every convert.

A great many people repudiate what has been put before them as the Christian Gospel.

They have never been able to see how good is the true Good News.

10 December

UNCOMPLICATED

Good news is surely not to be rejected merely because it *is* good!

Let us be on our guard against that common human tendency to elaborate a simple issue.

Compare, for example, the directness of Christ's words to the thief on the cross, 'today shalt thou be with me in Paradise', or Paul's plain statement that death only means 'to be with Christ, which is far better', with the enormous over-elaboration of Newman's *Dream of Gerontius*. Yet Newman's work is greatly admired, while Paul's conviction is scarcely taken seriously.

We who call ourselves Christians, should be continually vigilant against those who would darken counsel by complicating the simplicity of our faith. We need to be aware even of the religious books we read, or before long the simple walk with God becomes such a complicated spiritual exercise that the Good News ceases to be good.

I do not claim that Christianity is easy.

I do claim that it is not complicated.

11 December

GOD-SPEL

I believe that it is high time for the word 'Gospel' to be rehabilitated. It is a fine strong word with an interesting ancestry.

Back in the days of Homer, the Greek word *euaggelion* meant the reward given to the bringer of good news. Then its meaning changed over the centuries to denote, not the reward, but the good news itself. It was ripe for adoption by the New Testament writers, who invested it with a special importance. Instead of meaning any sort of good news, it was used to mean the Good News of God, the Christian Gospel. And with that specialized meaning it came into our language through the Old English god-spel.

But in common speech in latter years, the special meaning of the word has been blurred by loose usage. It is employed to mean almost any kind of teaching, idea, remedy or programme. Thus we may read of the 'gospel' of hard work, the 'gospel' of success, the 'gospel' of a salt-free diet or even the 'gospel' of Communism.

The word needs rescuing before it is further debased.

In Christian circles, we must see that what purports to be the Christian Gospel is always, and in the best sense, Good News.

✛

12 December

UNIQUE FACT

We all deplore the fact that the Advent season has become so highly commercialized, but it is difficult to see what we can do about it.

It is painful for Christians to see the original birthday celebration smothered under trappings and decoration, so that its religious significance is overlaid by purely pagan merry-making. But most painful, and indeed most dangerous, is the fact that millions of men and women regard the Christmas story as a beautifully preserved piece of folklore. They make no real distinction in their minds between the myth of Father Christmas and his reindeer, and the story of the babe with the adoring shepherds.

Christians can serve no good or useful purpose by decrying the generosity, the truce to normal hostility and the general goodwill engendered at Christmas-time. Indeed, though they are superficial, these things are often good. But wherever opportunity occurs, they must not hesitate to say that what we are celebrating is much more than this. It is a unique fact of human history.

13 December

GOD WITH US

I believe in the virgin birth.

It may seem strange to us that Luke, who was Paul's close companion, did not apparently tell him of Jesus' miraculous birth. Possibly Luke did not yet know this intimate secret. Perhaps it was not until he made his own personal investigations in Palestine that he learned the truth. God became man.

Jesus was not God pretending to be a man or acting a temporary part as a man. He became a real human being, as we are human beings, and he lived life on the same terms that we do. He enjoyed no special privilege or supernatural advantage. He drank to the last bitter drop the cup which he was asked to drink.

Life never is and never can be one prolonged Christmas party. The good cheer of Christmas is not the cards, the carols, the lighted Christmas tree, the holly and the ivy, the feasting, the presents. The real and lasting cause for joy is that God became a man like us. There can be no situation where he is not with us and in us.

He was so rightly called Immanuel or 'God with us'.

✤

14 December

THE CHRIST WHO ALWAYS WAS

Christ did not come into being when the Virgin Mary gave birth to a son. He existed before all time.

We read in St John's Gospel that 'in the beginning was the Word and the Word was God'. We also read that Christ is the force behind all creation, for 'by him were all things made and without him was not anything made that was made'.

There are a number of New Testament passages which bear witness to the pre-existence of Christ. The early Church had to defend her faith by pointing to this clear teaching when she met people who considered Christ merely an inspired prophet or as an ordinary man specially 'adopted' by God for his purpose.

We meet these tendencies today too in many places. Which of us has not heard people say that they respect Christ as a man, but cannot accept him as the eternal Son of God?

We should remind such people that they are flying directly in the face of what is plainly taught in the New Testament.

Look up these references—1 John 1:1; Ephesians 3:9; Colossians 1:16.

They tell us something about the Christ who is—and was.

✛

15 December

THE GOD WITH WHOM WE HAVE TO DO

There was a time when the orthodox Christian could not bear to think that Jesus was truly human, and subject to all the normal pressures and temptations, disappointments, griefs and fears. Today the pendulum has swung rather the other way. The *humanity* of Jesus (as shown so powerfully in Dennis Potter's TV play *Son of Man*) is pressed at the expense of his divinity.

No doubt it is a great and holy mystery but the fact is that Jesus was God *and* man. What we celebrate at Christmas is this deep and astonishing act in history by which God emptied himself of his divine attributes and deliberately plunged into the storm and stress of human living.

It is true that today the babe of Bethlehem is our risen and ascended Lord to whom all power belongs, and to whom eventually every knee shall bow. But in a story begun on the first Christmas Day, we get glimpse after glimpse of the nature of the God with whom we have to do.

Isn't it wonderful?

16 December

HE EMPTIED HIMSELF

There is a well-known passage in the New Testament that we all ought to know by heart. It is the only passage in the New Testament that gives any 'theological' description of that act of incarnation.

Let this mind be in you which was also in Christ Jesus: who, being in the form of God, thought it not a prize to be grasped at to be equal with God, but made himself of no reputation and took upon him the form of a servant and was made in the likeness of men: and being found in fashion as a man he humbled himself, and became obedient unto death, even the death of the cross.

PHILIPPIANS 2:5–8

These words 'being in the form of God' are much more important than they seem. The Greek word translated 'being' implies preexistence—the very thing on which St John is so insistent. The word translated 'form' means Christ was really and actually God at the very time that he became man.

Look at this phrase: 'made himself of no reputation' in verse 7.

It means *literally* 'he emptied himself'.

He did.

17 December

CLOSE RELATIONSHIP

Jesus Christ put aside, as it were, his divine attributes when he became man.

274

For instance, he put aside omniscience (the knowledge of everything) for he had to ask questions on several occasions, and as a child he learnt.

He put aside omnipresence (the ability to be in all places at the same time) for he manifestly was only in one place at a time.

He put aside omnipotence (the power of doing anything, almighty power) for he suffered wicked men to put him to death.

Yet he was really and truly God. His relationship to his Father was so close and his humanity so perfect that he never erred in any judgment or truth which he declared.

Jesus himself claimed that he and his Father were one, that he could forgive sins, that he was coming again in judgment—and a host of other things which no one who was not God could legitimately claim.

No one could read the Gospels without realizing that Jesus claimed for himself nothing less than divinity.

✤

18 December

TAKE OFF THE MASK!

It must be of the deepest possible concern to all of us who profess and call ourselves Christians to communicate the enormous significance of God's visit. Indeed, it may well be that, before we can attempt any such communication, we need ourselves to think far more deeply about the meaning of an event which many of us have known and accepted since we were children.

Possibly we have forgotten, through very familiarity, that what we sometimes so lightly call the 'incarnation,' is by far the most important single fact of human history.

The mask which Christmas wears in our minds may be neither that of commercialization nor of irrational rejoicing, but we should gain very greatly in our effectiveness as Christians if we stripped off the mask of traditional acceptance and saw, with new eyes, the marvel of God's visit.

The world's problems are far greater and more complex than any our forefathers knew. Our conception of God himself is vastly greater than that even of our grandfathers.

This in one way makes our traditional belief in the incarnation harder, but in another way, it means that the personal coming of God into human history is of far deeper and wider implication than any previous generation has had the chance to imagine.

❖

19 December

TIDINGS OF JOY

'Let good Christian men rejoice!' But again let us know in heart and mind *why* we rejoice!

Many around us will enjoy themselves behind the many masks of Christmas. But they will relapse into joylessness, fear and anxiety unless the One whose birthday we celebrate becomes to them real, alive, and contemporary.

It is we who are Christians who hold the secret behind the façade, but it was never meant to be a secret. On the contrary, from the beginning it was meant to be 'good tidings of great joy which shall be to all people'.

By thought, by prayer, by every tried and untried means, let us do all that we possibly can to make known that astonishing mystery, which is also a historical fact, that God became one of us so that we might become like him.

20 December

BACKWARDS TO CHRISTMAS

In a sense, the early Christians looked backward to Christmas. Most of them, we may safely guess, knew in experience the reconciliation wrought by his death and the power released by his resurrection before they ever heard the strange story of his humble birth. But not many generations passed before Christians were celebrating with every kind of human rejoicing the heart and centre of their faith—that God became Man.

In the fourth century Constantine, the first Christian Roman emperor, for good or ill, decreed that the pagan festival of the winter solstice should be combined with the Church's celebration of the nativity of her Lord. From that time onwards, and perhaps with growing confusion, there has been a mixture of pagan jollification and Christian rejoicing.

That is why every Christmas, we must deliberately and thoughtfully look *backwards*.

21 December

AS GOOD AS A PLAY

Although it looks nice on a Christmas card, it is not really much fun to put your baby to sleep in a horse's feeding-trough because there is nowhere else except the dirty floor.

It is a dreadful thing for a mother to feel that the world has no room for her baby.

How it must have cheered Mary when the rough shepherds came bursting in, all breathless and excited, saying that they had had a vision of angels up there on the hillside and had been told beyond all doubt that this little fellow was really God.

Might they please kneel and give him their presents!

How the people snoring comfortably in the inn next door would have laughed to have seen the sight of the shepherds kneeling on the stable floor!

Why, it was as good as a play!

But that is how God made *his* entrance.

✛

22 December

OUT OF BETHLEHEM

It may well have been a very shame-faced and embarrassed innkeeper who offered Joseph and Mary the only shelter he had available. It was poor indeed but it was dry and warm in the company of the beasts of the farm.

'No room in the inn' is a phrase which, if we are not careful, conveys the idea to us of a harassed desk-clerk at an admittedly third-rate country inn saying to the anxious Joseph, 'Sorry, sir, but all the rooms are booked!' But the eastern inn (or *khan*) in a village like Bethlehem was nothing like the poorest of modern inns. And the statement that there was 'no room' means literally that there was no 'place' or 'space' on the earthen floor of that grossly overcrowded little resting-place for travellers.

We do not know who first thought of the 'stable' or 'lean-to' or 'cave' where the animals were brought in for the night, but lowly as it was, it gave the holy young woman, whom God had chosen for this unique honour, shelter, warmth and privacy. And who amidst the snoring or revelling crowd next door could have guessed what was happening a few yards away?

To me, marvel of marvels, who told Micah, the prophet of nearly seven centuries before, that out of negligible little Bethlehem should come the Ruler and Shepherd of God's people? (Micah 5:2).

23 December

NO FAIRY TALE

God was born in very humble circumstances—he was, as the hymn puts it, born 'in a lowly cattle shed'.

The actual event was far from romantic. There is nothing gay and amusing about a young woman having to hunt desperately for some shelter where she could give birth to her first child.

On that first Christmas morning, the world must have seemed a hard place to Mary. At the end of a weary journey there was 'no room at the inn'.

The only shelter offered to her was the 'lowly cattle shed'.

I find this a great mystery and a great wonder. Every day science discovers more and more of the complex wisdom of God. Anyone who uses his mind has a much bigger idea of God than our grandfathers, or even our fathers, ever had. Yet God has been here on this planet, in person.

What we are celebrating this week is not the feast of jolly old Father Christmas or good King Wenceslas, or a beautiful fairy-tale.

We are celebrating the visit of God.

How marvellous!

24 December

THE WISDOM OF GOD

The incredibly humble entry of God into his own world is not at all what we might have expected. Indeed we may be shocked that such a tremendous event should have happened in such poverty and such obscurity as we have described.

Consider how the nativity might have been planned today!

Think of the careful preparation, the special arrangement beforehand! And then, when the event actually took place and the child was born, can we imagine the reporters, the world news coverage, the interviews, the microphones and the TV cameras!

But God's ways are not our ways. Although this was God entering his own world, he enjoyed no special privilege or protection. As the hymn rightly says, 'With the poor and mean and lowly, lived on earth our Saviour holy'.

The world in which we live today teaches us to value things, success and wealth and glamour and power, above all. But we shall look in vain for any of these things in the true facts of Christmas. There is a sublime simplicity and a heart-stirring beauty in the events we see in Bethlehem.

We look, apparently, at a helpless baby, newborn in the humblest surroundings.

It is hard to believe he is the Son of God.

The longer I live the more I grow convinced that the apparent weakness of Jesus is really tremendous strength. In the end it will become plain that there is no true success except in following his way, no beauty apart from the character he showed us, no power except the power of his love.

God's wisdom is a far higher thing than ours.

25 December

THE KING WHO MUST REIGN

Jesus was born, as we said, in a 'lowly cattle shed' that is in the outhouse of a village inn. Who amid all the excitement and noise of a reunion of friends and relations (even though it was compulsory) had the slightest idea that within a few yards of them the Word had become flesh?

But this is the way of God.

His 'weakness' is greater than our strength and his 'foolishness' greater than all our wisdom. Even our pride, our hatred, our fear, and our selfishness cannot defeat his unfailing love.

The baby lying in the manger seemed as frail and helpless as any other scrap of human life. Yet he grew into a Man of matchless quality, a Man of such tempered strength that even death could not hold him.

The baby we worship today is now alive eternally, both in our hearts and beyond time-and-space, the King who must reign.

❖

26 December

NEW MEANING

Christianity gave the word 'love' a new and deeper meaning. The new kind of love was stimulated and developed by accepting the love of God as shown in Christ, the babe of Bethlehem, the King of kings.

'If God so loved us, we ought also to love one another,' wrote John.

The new life of faith and hope is made possible according to Paul 'because the love of God is shed abroad in our hearts'.

❖

27 December

LOOK FORWARD

A friend of mine, who worked as a writer in London, suddenly collapsed at his desk. His companions hurriedly telephoned a doctor, since to all appearances my friend, who is in his forties, looked as if he had had a severe heart attack and was perhaps already dead. But he was not. The doctor, who arrived as soon as he could, diagnosed 'nervous exhaustion', and had the patient sent home for rest and recovery.

Naturally I wrote a letter as soon as I knew of this happening, and offered what hope and encouragement I could. But his letter in reply surprised me.

I knew the man to be a very fine Christian, but I thought there would be some hint of, if not self-pity, regret that the days of great activity of mind were apparently suddenly cut short. On the contrary, the new situation was a new opportunity of doing God's will even under severe handicap.

Here was no 'lamenting for past raptures' (to borrow C.S. Lewis' phrase) but a hopeful looking forward to the exploring of a new phase of life.

Knowing the man, I am sure that this was no mere putting up of a bold front. It was a simple, and highly courageous, acceptance of a future largely unknown.

It made me feel small, for how often I longed for the health and vitality that once I had, and how often have I gracelessly accepted present limitations?

I am sure my friend's hopeful forward-looking attitude is right.

❖

28 December

FOR GOOD?

How can it be true that 'all things work together for good…' even in this topsy-turvy world… 'for *those who love God*'?

Because the inward attitude of the man who loves God is so different that, without breaking any of the rules that he himself has made, God is able to bring good to that man even out of evil and pain.

The man who does not love God is really in love with himself, his position, his success, his pleasure. He may be lucky or unlucky, but by no conceivable effort can he accept all that life may bring and turn it to good account. For it may bring him failure and disappointment, ill-health and loss, and 'what will the robin do then, poor thing?'

The man who loves God is in an unassailable position. He has surrendered his own plans to the greater permanent plan of God, the responsibility for which is God's. He asks no favours of God but he does ask for the guiding and strength of God that, through him, God's will may be achieved.

There is nothing now that can happen which cannot be turned into good for him.

For all things *do* work together for good.

✤

29 December

PRESS ON!

The old Roman god Janus, from whom we get the name of the month of January, was often represented as having two faces, one facing forwards and one backwards. Like the ancient Romans, we are inclined to look backwards as well as forward at the threshold of the New Year.

Is there any point in looking back? Is it not all past history, gone beyond recall? Yes, it is; but if we seriously believe in God and his purpose in the world, it is useful to look back. We can at least see our own mistakes and failures. We can look back in genuine thankfulness to God, and remind ourselves that he remains the same whatever the unknown future may bring.

But we must never be tied to the past or spend our lives bewailing the years that are gone for ever. St Paul declares that 'forgetting the things that are past' he 'presses on' to carry out God's purpose for him (Philippians 3:13–14). St Paul had accepted God's forgiveness after sincere repentance, and he was not going to allow past evils to haunt the present or spoil the future.

The same attitude should be ours.

We may allow ourselves a glance back now and again, but don't live in the past.

Don't go over and over old sins that, once they are forgiven, may be safely forgotten.

The two-faced god never did live.

At most he was an image held in men's minds at the year's opening.

Our God is living and active.

He calls us onwards in courage and hope.

Press on!

✣

30 December

GOD'S TRUTH

As we enter the New Year we need not so much resolution as realization.

'Beloved,' wrote St John long ago, 'now are we the sons of God.' The men of old did not deserve such an honour and neither do we, but it makes a world of difference to our attitude towards life if we say (if necessary again and again) *now are we the sons of God*'. For we are his workmanship, his responsibility, even his pride and joy. We are not striving to please some remote 'infinitude'. God is with us and in us, working ceaselessly to make us into men and women of better quality.

Far more use than making any number of resolutions would be to take time off and quietly realize what God is trying to do and to see how we can co-operate.

Think again on these familiar words:

'The Kingdom of God is within you' (Luke 17:21).

'Strengthened with might by his Spirit in the inner man' (Ephesians 3:16).

'It is God which worketh in you both to will and to do (Philippians 2:13).

'He which hath begun a good work in you will perform it' (Philippians 1:6).

'Greater is he that is in you than he that is in the world' (1 John 4:4).
'Behold, I make all things new' (Revelation 21:5).
This is God's truth.

❖

31 December

THE FUTURE

What about the future?

Nobody knows anything for sure about it. There is no guarantee against accident, illness, bereavement or, at the end of this little life, death. We are wise if we recognize this, and face life as it is, and not as we want it to be.

We shall be saved much heartbreak if we stop forever expecting what we would call 'fair' or 'just'. Frequently the innocent suffer and evil men prosper. This has been the pattern since the world began.

It is not, of course, the *final* answer, for that we cannot see in this world, but in the present tangled field of human life, both good and evil 'grow together until the harvest'.

The Christian has such an advantage as he faces a new year. He knows that *nothing in life, however painful or distressing, can ever separate him from the love of God.*

Always, at all times, waking and sleeping, he is held in that unfailing love.

As John Greenleaf Whittier put it so rightly, 'I only know I cannot drift beyond his love and care.'

❖

In face of all this, what is there left to say? If God is for us, who can be against us? He who did not grudge his own Son but gave him up for us all—can we not trust such a God to give us, with him, everything else that we can need?

Who can separate us from the love of Christ? Can trouble, pain or persecution? Can lack of clothes and food, danger to life and limb, the threat of force of arms?

No, in all these things we win an overwhelming victory through him who has proved his love for us.

ROMANS 8:31–37

THE WORKS OF DR J.B. PHILLIPS

NEW TESTAMENT TRANSLATIONS

1947 *Letters to Young Churches*, William Collins (Fontana 1971)
1952 *The Gospels in Modern English*, William Collins (Fontana 1971)
1955 *The Young Church in Action*, William Collins (Fontana 1971)
1957 *The Book of Revelation*, William Collins
1958 *The New Testament in Modern English*, William Collins

OTHER BOOKS

1952 *Your God is Too Small*, Epworth Press
1952 *Making Men Whole*, Epworth Press (Fontana 1971)
1954 *Plain Christianity*, Epworth Press
1954 *Appointment with God*, Epworth Press
1954 *When God Was Man*, Lutterworth Press
1956 *New Testament Christianity*, Hodder and Stoughton
1956 *The Church Under the Cross*, Highway Press
1956 *St Luke's Life of Christ*, William Collins
1957 *Is God at Home?*, Lutterworth Press
1957 *God With Us*, Epworth Press
1959 *A Man Called Jesus*, William Collins
1960 *God Our Contemporary*, Hodder and Stoughton
1960 *Good News*, William Collins
1961 *The Christian Year*, William Collins
1963 *Four Prophets*, William Collins
1967 *Ring of Truth*, Hodder and Stoughton

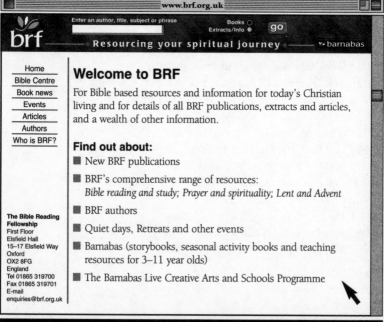

www.brf.org.uk

Enter an author, title, subject or phrase

Books ○
Extracts/Info ●

go

brf

Resourcing your spiritual journey — barnabas

Home
Bible Centre
Book news
Events
Articles
Authors
Who is BRF?

The Bible Reading Fellowship
First Floor
Elsfield Hall
15–17 Elsfield Way
Oxford
OX2 8FG
England
Tel 01865 319700
Fax 01865 319701
E-mail
enquiries@brf.org.uk

Welcome to BRF

For Bible based resources and information for today's Christian living and for details of all BRF publications, extracts and articles, and a wealth of other information.

Find out about:

■ New BRF publications

■ BRF's comprehensive range of resources:
Bible reading and study; Prayer and spirituality; Lent and Advent

■ BRF authors

■ Quiet days, Retreats and other events

■ Barnabas (storybooks, seasonal activity books and teaching resources for 3–11 year olds)

■ The Barnabas Live Creative Arts and Schools Programme

Visit the BRF website at www.brf.org.uk